1-800-I AM-UNHAPPY

Volume 2

inspirational writs by

CHRIS BENT

Published in the USA by
Chris Bent
Naples, Florida
USA

http://ChrisBent.com

ISBN 978-0-9913328-1-6

DEDICATION

To Christina, Candice, Courtney, and their journeys . . .

Prologue

This is meant to be a book for just one person. If just that one person is touched in some way to make their journey better, then the effort is not in vain. Each one of us can look back to one moment that changed our direction for the better. May this book, a collection of my writs and wit, find that pair of eyes.

Chris Bent

Kennebunkport
September 2013
www.ChrisBent.com

Contents

This book is meant to be different and a little strange.
It was never planned. I had written what I call a few "writs"
over the last 10 years. Short pieces that just came in a moment.
I often would get up in the middle of the night and write…
Most all are done in 30 minutes. Go figure?
Where does it come from? I don't know it just flows.
I never knew where the next sentence would go.
I think they are very funny while being as deep as you wish to
go…Each chapter is short, mostly only 500 words
so you can pick up at any time.
These are reflections on our times today and all the challenges
facing us, especially our children…It is your journey…hope I help.
1-800-1 AM-UNHAPPY

inspirational writs by

CHRIS BENT

"Shot Across the Bow"

A shot across the bow is a warning to slow down and stop so you may be boarded and searched for something dangerous.

Schools are such easy targets. We all have known about bullies in our neighborhoods and schools all our lives. A bully is someone who is insecure and angry at not feeling accepted in socially acceptable groups. The parents were called, the bully was disciplined, hopefully embarrassed, and kicked out of school at the next provocation. In my days the Principal took me down into the coal room and spanked me with a paddle. Problem solved.

Today's tragedy in Newtown, CT is abominable, hurtful, and embarrassing. But the tears don't give a damn. These are the innocent of the innocent's lives lost. I write and I write about core America. About values retreating into politically correct safe rooms. This majority remains silent except for some letters to the editors. The liberal press does

not talk about values as that would mean defining what is good and what is evil. It has been left to our politically correct judicial system to refine into fine print.

Don't we get it? Hello? We have abrogated our very reason for being to well funded special interests. Fear of confrontation, both verbal and legal, forces us to find other things to do.

Concurrently, we have the insidious cultural byproduct of new technologies. Facebook, texting, Twitter, and video games are providing the new ego development infrastructure. When a kid spends hours playing combat games, evil and death are just video screen deep. Pavlovian conditioning at its finest. Think about it. "Am I OK? Are you OK?" is texted all day long. Reassurance is instant not earned. Play is no longer outside, it is inside… inside the brain.

Then we have the breakdown of traditions, traditional values…disparaged by the new sensitivities. What is there to fall back on??? What is there to fall back on when dad leaves when you are six years old??? Visitation rights. Really helpful.

Churches are being mocked as offering nothing but confusion while the video screen promises truth and knowledge and reality shows. 60 Minute analysis of religion delights in exposing hypocrisy rather than miraculous transformations of the lost.

Enter the newborn. Enter the sick kid who feels left out and is angry that he does not have all to which he is entitled. In the video game bodies drop. You win if you reach a certain level.

Who won today at Sandy Hook?

Why is non-faith better than faith? Who says?

"Blameless"

It is so sad. Beyond senseless. How deep can despair go? Innocence defiled.

What is evil? Biblical baloney.

There has to be something to blame. That is the key question. For once discovered and analyzed remedies can be legalized. Then our nation, re-self assured, can reclaim paradise. But... evil, which we pretend cannot really exist, won't go away. It remains the same even with modern technology, legal excellence and, of course, political savvy.

Once we have exhausted gun legislation and psycho-medical infrastructure refinement we, if we open our eyes, will remain on square one. Evil does not go away. The majority will continue to pretend otherwise.

What to do? Time to kneel and pray again? Time to look up and ponder the imponderable with humility and grace. For only hope and community can provide a path. Returning to old values and abandoned dignities.

"Blood on the floor is not a game."

Precious time between parents and child, school and student, government and governed must be purged of the enabling equivocations. We permit too much. We do not oversee enough. We are not physically present enough. Love in person cannot be replaced by gifts and freedom. Youth need the continuum of security, peace, and love. Family must look inward again. Family must be values driven again. At all costs.

Newtown, Utoya, Aleppo are places now defined by evil. The list of evil events goes back for millenniums as it will go forward for millenniums. The WTC in lower Manhattan will fade into historical obscurity as will all these others. But not evil. It remains the adversary. It is real not imagined. Blood on the floor is not a game.

Solution demanded. Who says it is not our war? Our problem is that we seek answers in a computer and not on our knees.

"Legally Insane"

Have we become legally insane???

I know it is insane to write this. Some of you are already reaching for your phone… Because when you hear someone say something not funny or even funny these days you had better be on the safe side and report it. We will never know who is calling about whom. The telephone control room for the first responders will always be hiring. On the application just say you know how to use a phone. Oops… someone is knocking at my door.

Please do not think I am talking about mental illness. That is for the experts. However, regulations are in the works to define all forms of insanities and how to carefully respond to them in appropriate stages so everyone involved in the process is on legally sound ground. Real fine print kinda ground. Of course, as a matter of obvious logic, each of these steps will have to be signed off on by three supervisors… Once this infrastructure is in place there will

"Am I nuts?"

be a group from both Houses who will have to determine what the boundaries will be. Will they be defined by acts, intents, or words? Thresholds for relevancy fleshed out etc. I am sure this will require only a minimum of debate.

Unfortunately, there is no way to keep good and bad out of this discussion. They will also have to be re-defined in light of 21st century realities. I hope that evil is passed over or it could extend these determinations. All must be completely recorded, transposed, and cross checked for veracity by a select committee of savvy politicians and attorneys.

Then, of course, it will have to be voted on by the individual states and endorsed by a Supreme Court when contested.

Ok, once good and bad is sorted out, we have to address new bedrock values as the old ones are the ones that got us into trouble in the first place. Values. What values do you hold dear? Are they prioritized for the sake of analysis efficiency? Then we have to take everyone's values and collate them with a prioritizing factor. This has to be done legally and reviewed at appropriate junctures.

Am I nuts? Why have we legally bound ourselves to fine print? Where is a handshake and trust? Where?

There is an old adage that says "Just do it and apologize later." I like it. Caution: Data mining will pop this up and codify me as potentially subversive.

This is insane. Is it legal to be insane? Or is it insane to be legal???

"Guilt Trip"

There has to be this fabulous island one can voyage to in complete peace where the diving is great, the people are embracing, and the food sublime. Guilt-Free Island in Micronesia, the South Pacific. Takes a long time to get there but it is truly worth it.

For a brief period just after birth before our mother's first "no" we were on that island. Ever since guilt has roamed our persona creating havoc with our insecurities and self-image, other acquaintances and friends and families also have had their own unique swirl of hidden guilts. This is going on all around us. Who ever knows what the truth really is as guilt agendas influence every conversation?

What is the source of this disturbance, guilt?

Is it not because you feel you did something wrong? What is wrong with wrong? How did you determine what was wrong? Was it because someone else said so? Can you trust their judgment, or was it driven by guilt?

> *"That is your journey and your choice."*

Life's quest is about finding out who we really are. You hear the expression "find yourself." How do you do that? How do you know who you are anyway??? Ok, by talking to friends and seeing if you are accepted. Ok, but how do you know they are right and who are they really??? So how do you find out what you believe? We have to believe something??? Hello??? Is life not a video game… or endless entertainment…

So once again, something has to mean something including you. When you feel that little guilt pang it is signaling something is not right. What to do to make it go away??? Not a drink, not a drug, not entertainment… no…they are all short term and don't do the job and you have to start all over again….

Doing something good does make a difference and guilt gets pushed aside. Do good all the time and… voila!… No guilt. That simple… think about it.

How do you know what is good? Values. You have to have values by which to determine good. Where do you find values?

I know. But I am not telling you. That is your journey and your choice. But when you get there you will know it and know it was worth the exhausting and perilous effort. Guilt trip.

"Respect"

It was 9:30 AM today, December 21, 2012 and our employees and I held hands in silence, a national moment of respect for a great loss of innocence.

Some of us, I really wished it were all of us, could say this was a moment of prayer. Prayer to an invisible God we know in faith is there. But the word prayer is shunned by those who choose to believe otherwise. I cannot see how there can be hope without faith. How you can be "lucky" rather than "blessed".

A moment of respect. Respect is also becoming a diluted concept. A person can be making a point in a dignified manner and anyone can now stand up and yell and scream their opposition.

A child now more often answers a parent with a "whatever".

A celebrity is pulled over and dismissively tells the officer "MY lawyer will handle this…"

A clergy implies a Biblical reference and is mocked.

Values are now the target of sarcasm. Is the Tomb of the Unknown Soldier too militaristic? This is where we are heading.

Respect? What is there of value anymore? What should we respect? Parents? The law? Money? Fun? Right to do anything we want?

Is sacrosanct now a ridiculous concept?

Don't mess with my Facebook, my texts, my tweets... The new sacrosanct???

Respect my right to my communications, my music, and my videos. Then we can talk. I will respect your feelings.

Meanwhile, kneel for Newtown.

"No Problem"

Why say "No problem" if there is no problem??? Everywhere you go these days and you request someone to do something or just to answer you get a "No problem." Huuuhh??? What??? To say "No problem" you are inferring that there could have been but you have taken care of it already... Huuuhh??? What??? Can someone please clue me in as to why there are so many new problems that are so easily remedied by a "No problem???"

When the Captain gives the Lieutenant an order does he expect a "No problem sir"??? Don't you see that the "No problem" responder takes control of the moment? It is really a new defense mechanism to claim no responsibility and an undertone of dismissiveness. Well... I have lost you... OK... No problem.

But whatever happened to "Yes"??? Does just saying a simple "Yes" indicate weakness? Acquiescence in a

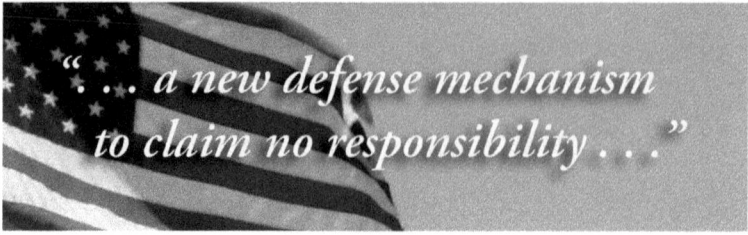

"... a new defense mechanism to claim no responsibility ..."

world which so protects sensitivities??? What are we afraid of admitting? It must be that to say "Yes" you have relinquished some sort of control. Why must there be a debate before anyone can say "Yes"?

What about that phrase of contemporary derision... "Yes sir"? You can't say "sir" because old fashioned manners are no longer in vogue or it is racist. What about "Yes ma'am"??? Think the same thing applies. No problem.

How about I ask you some questions befitting of a "no problem" response.

Do you like your parents?

May I take you to McDonalds?

Are there any things you believe in?

What are they?

Is there a difference between indifference and insecurity?

Is there a difference between good and evil?

Do you know how stimulating and reassuring it is to have one say "No problem" to you???

Get a life and be a problem to those who deserve problems.

"Cartoon"

Isn't a cartoon wonderful? Especially the strip ones in the newspaper. You know you are going to get a chuckle and a thought to which you can nod in assent. Gosh, isn't that the truth…? Chuckle… Of course there are the action ones, the romance ones… but the chuckle ones are the best.

The way society is behaving these days makes me chuckle. We are repeating the same mistakes over and over. No one cares about history any more. I chuckle at that.

I would love to line up all the year's political cartoons on a really big wall and get a really big chuckle. So funny. Fiscal cliff cartoons are scary as they make fun of a potential big fall. The government should be handing out winged parachute suits so we can get as far away as possible. But like everything else the government hands out there are so many forms and fine print that you really need a tandem suit so your lawyer can be attached to your, you know… What a cartoon!

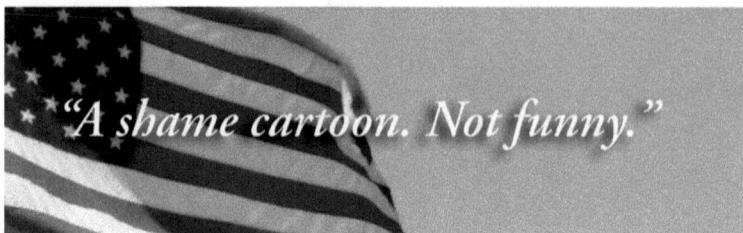

When was the last time you really had a good chuckle?
I wish we could all share them. But maybe we are…
as so many people are texting all the time, maybe the
walking and driving without looking up means they are
chuckling??? LOL…

I bet the police get a chuckle when they see more and more
cars swerving back into position as the heads arise. We
need police chuckle statistics to get a handle on the chuckle
epidemic.

Now what is going on with international women's rights is
not a chuckle. It is almost certainly a cartoon when all the
buffoons and selfish characters out there have made justice
and fairness into a cartoon noir. A shame cartoon. Rulers
and politicians have turned causes into shame cartoons. Not
funny. Chuckleless. And they are clueless.

What if all the cartoon writers banded together with an
agenda making certain months or weeks subject specific?
Cause specific. This could spur unified chuckles that

could be heard around the world and get moving on cause reduction. Cartoon power!!!

How about we also confront the seven deadliest and shame them. Let's make fun of evil. Now that is a chuckle.

"CO2"

I have a friend, Philippe, who believes that CO2 is our number one priority. The misfortunes and indecisions of man come to foot at this group of elements. Hmm…

When I was a kid, you know… mid 20's… the Navy taught to me swim at night by using the Emerson Closed Circuit Rebreather. It gave off no bubbles so no one knew you were swimming under their ship to attach a limpet mine that would go off long after you had swum away. There was this chemical called baralyme, a mixture of calcium and barium that acted as a CO2 absorbent in a filter that was part of the breathing path. The problem was that if water leaked in then the baralyme would not absorb the CO2 which was toxic. Then you would rebreathe it and die.

So we did not like CO2. We liked living. Well, our planet does not like excessive CO2 and we should be finding ways to filter and reduce it. Let's have the North and South poles happy again.

"We are the pollutant."

At the same time I wish all this CO2 fervor could be channeled into all kinds of other issues like cruelty to humans. We have the SPCA. Where is the SPCH? Where do these politicians and leaders (choke) in all these other countries have the gall to watch their citizens suffer and die while they are having great meals every night??? Shame on the many that treat women like animals. Where is the SPCW?

Why are we and all our media not crying out in rage at these even more pressing tragedies? Why do we ignore the torture and abject denial of human rights and dignity in North Korea, much less the Middle East… and all the other places that are protected by political correctness?

Why? Is CO2 poisoning already creeping into our bodies??? Why is our judgment so impaired? What has happened to our values??? We don't have to bomb… but where is our outrage? Why are we always apologizing? Come on America.

Do you believe in anything? Do we just withdraw from the truth until the next major war? How come our veterans and servicemen are so patriotic? What do they see that we don't?

Why are they silent when they return…? Is it because they don't think we can understand? Or care???

They know values. Do we? Values are the cornerstone of our democratic society. They have been forged in blood and sacrifice for centuries. And now we act as if they were archaic principles not that relevant to our digital age. That our Judeo-Christian Constitution is old parchment riddled with holes and outdated irrelevancies.

Our problem is not with the environment, it is with us. We individuals do not make our individual stands. We are asking government to take responsibility for all our needs rather than forging them out of collective individualism. Each of us squanders. Each of us is responsible. My dad always said, "Turn out the lights Chris." I do to this day. But we could watch all that we do. Use less energy. Become energy efficient. Become values efficient. We need to manage our own details.

We don't look as healthy as we used to. We have legislated so much out of what should be normal. Where are the afternoon athletics in schools? Where are the values in schools? Let's blame ourselves in a courageous act of accountability without hurting feelings… LOL.

The endangered is man. We are the pollutant. God help us.

"Diophobia"

When I was a kid my dad put this large black snake in my arms and it scared me… So I am not fond of snakes… but I have outgrown the fear… maybe it was a phobia once???

I loved it when girls screamed when you said "Mouse!" So funny. They have all these phobias.

Go to Wikipedia and you will find an infinite number of them… Just a few of the "A's": Algophobia — Fear of pain, Amphobia — Fear of garlic, Allodoxaphobia — Fear of opinions, Altophobia - Fear of heights, Amathophobia - Fear of dust, Amaxophobia - Fear of riding in a car. You get the idea… but there must be 1000 of them and growing. We find new labels for new fears all the time. I'll make one up: Textphobic… someone has to be afraid of texting… or it could be a label for older people who don't text. Label them and you can dismiss them. It seems like more and more people (especially the younger) like to classify and label people or ideas they don't understand or don't make the effort to try to understand.

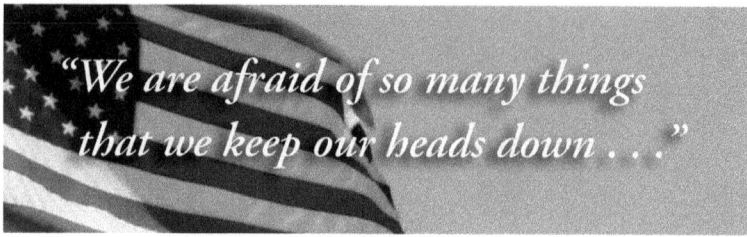

Take history. Nobody seems to find relevancy or guidance from history today. We have so much going on that is new and time demanding that leaving the past in the dust is reasonable if not smart. Not. Historiphobic we have become. I just made that up.

This is going to get not-funny real quick now... Truphobic can be our aversion to Truth. Many who have wasted so much of their lives are afraid of the Truth. It takes rehab and sharing to surmount the citadels of denial.

Go ahead and Google phobias and see how many are applicable to you and us. We are afraid of so many things that we keep our heads down as we text for solutions. If we don't look up, life will pass us by...

These last years have seen blaming and labeling metastasize. Campaigns of fear and demonizing to curry constituencies. Self-serving half-truth advertising to sell product, ideology, and emotional uncertainties that undercut our moral cornerstones. That's a big sentence. Think about it. For in this din of fuzzy belief emerges uncertainty and an erosion of everything we used to hold dear.

Fear of chaos, chaophobia??? I hear more people thinking in this direction. Maybe it is a rational fear after all???

We strip values from our schools and replace them with ambiguous sensitivities. We celebrate directionless celebrity. We are redefining life in material terms. The new rational. "Newratophobia?"

We have a fear of anyone telling us what to do. We are Orderphobic.

Diophobia. We are afraid of anything that is of God. We are afraid of the concept, His name… you name it. The Bible is held as some form of heresy by most. But I just cannot escape the Truths written so thoroughly so many thousands of years ago.

How can all the laws and recommendations be so on target?

Why are we so afraid of God?

They threw stones at Jesus a long time ago. We haven't stopped. They hurt the same.

We should be afraid of ourselves.

"Opinions"

Letters to the Editor. Do you ever read them in your hometown newspaper? There seem to be so many more these days. How in the world does an editor edit the feelings of thousands? They used to be fun, for the most part... and you could laugh. Not at... but with... if you get what I am saying.

Opinions now are aimed at someone else. They are more like verbal bullets of complaint and derision. Bad analogy these days but the bullets of acrimony feed large magazines of pain. They should be banned? Verbal poisons of mass destruction. Nuances of camouflaged hate fill every other letter. Frustration and disappointment seem to be themes of protest. Opinion after opinion coming from a real person.

In my town the wisdom of years does not preclude real criticism from forming into trajectories of division. Great people are being sucked into this war of words. Opinions are now more than opinions... they are becoming "I dare you's". And we all know the next step...

"Opinions are trendy and in fashion."

Now suppose our brilliant national database was able to post the addresses of all "opinion"- ators???

Now I know my editor has high standards. Why else would 90% of my articles never see daylight? His rules and values set standards. Well, maybe there should be rules and standards for all opinions??? Bet we would sally up to that real fast. So where is freedom without rules and standards, much less values?

Where is respect and humility? I think the silent majority does not have an opinion. Of course, if they shared there would not be a newspaper big, oops... courageous enough to print them... because the silent majority is boring. Anyone with values is really boring. Anyone with real beliefs is soo boring.

Opinions are trendy and in fashion. They are so easy to toss out and blog ad nauseum. Gotta stay busy...

My dad said "Keep your opinion to yourself Chris." I hope he does not read this up in Heaven.

"Revolution"

1776 again??? Our backs were up against the wall with the rules and laws of the British. We yearned for freedoms, especially freedom of speech and religion. They were being boxed in. "Common Sense" prevailed. One thing led to another. Arms were borne. Freedom won.

So where is the thin line in the sand for freedoms? In the old days there was no information media really. Today we know so much that confusion rules and simplicity is lost. We are losing judgment to the margins of society. The right, the left… now it's the extreme right and the extreme left. All is marginalized. All is demonized. The labeling of labels has created a sea of ignorance and intolerance. Where in the heck are we?

Don't you wish you were back out on some farm somewhere where nature's brutal indifference was more acceptable? Where hot and cold is preferable to half truths and denial. Where flooding and wind is preferable to unemployment and uncertainty. Remember the "I can't stand it anymore" guy???

Is there not anyone in Washington who can't stand it anymore? Reconciliation or revolution are the options. The former is less certain. Let's have a big picnic in front of the Lincoln Memorial and get drunk so when we start shooting at each other we miss. I want a beer and wine revolution, not a social one. Maybe bows and arrows... Or even better... pumpkin catapults.

Seriously, our nation is in trouble. We have allowed and welcomed the demonization of us, we brothers. My brother has become my labeled enemy. He is tattooed with half truth. Forget the unparalleled injustices of the Middle East. Forget our abominable indifference to international women's rights... Forget all that... there is a whiff of real internal revolution in the air. Streets filled with protest looming. Protesters fighting protesters. Anger and mayhem that only troops, not executive order, can quell. Which side will take over the country?

This is 2013, not 1776... or is it?

"Counterintuitive Combat"

Cultural heritage is dead. Long live ambiguous ideology. What restricted us is no longer relevant. The truth has been liberated from the confines of former generations. Freedom is once again in the hands of the thinking man. Intuition is suspect. Rules and laws are not.

You see, I was raised to treat women with respect. I was taught to open the door for them. After all they are the bearers of birth. They mother and protect the child. Accordingly it is my instinct to protect women. I cannot avoid it any more than I can lust… (a little humor). You hit a woman and I am in your face. You are rude to a woman and I don't turn away. It is instinct.

War is ugly, frightening, and beyond inhuman. Men in combat stay in new trenches of extreme discomfort and uncertainty. Why do combat veterans on the ground never talk about what they have seen? Because you won't understand and he cannot summon the words to adequately

describe the horror. Weeks and months in exhausting conditions. Man was made to protect women. Just look at his body. Hello?

The current debate should be made and voted on only by people who have been in ground combat. This is their debate, not ours. I am all for female fighter pilots... they can be deadly. But just wait till one is beheaded in some Middle Eastern square. Then vote again.

The pundits of media are just that. Pun intended.

Why in the world is the war not on women's rights?! Why is it not being fought first? The inhumane treatment of women in "those" other cultures goes un-attacked. Where are the warrior pundits??? They should be ripping all regimes apart that condone their chauvinist insanities. Shame on them.

Women in combat? Hell, they are in prison over there begging to be rescued.

"Mind Control"

Mind control was a hypothesis experimented with during the Cold War. It has probably been tried for eons. You want to torture me and I am sure I can change some opinions. Or better… you want me to like and become familiar with something?… then run your ads on TV over and over. Or tell my mom I did something wrong. There are many ways to change thinking. Or you can affirm and reward me for doing what you wish. The mind begs to be changed until it knows who it is. Until it knows who it must be. Until it knows what it must protect… at all odds.

Some minds are out of control. In my mind, that is. When minds are out of control they need re-direction. But how??? We have to be so sensitive to sensitivities that we need laws that are perfect. We need rules that last and that have proven lastingness.

The debate has been who gets to set these laws? The parent? The guardian? The church? The county? The government? Gimme a break. Where are the right laws supposed to come from??? Help!!! Tilt!

"Can we go back and start over?"

We first have to settle who is the law maker. We are off in our media debating all kinds of options but cannot decide who the supreme ruler is… We cannot say we stand for anything anymore for fear of criticism from any quarter… however diminished… conundrum.

Revolution? Dissolution? Standards blurred. Solutions lost.

Can we go back and start over? Sure seems like we are headed nowhere but further into boring political quicksand. If the government's executives can't execute? If the leading minds of the media can't lead? Then how can unity be achieved other than brief moments after some hideous crisis…? Then we start all over and parse responsibility.

Maybe it is better to be a farmer with no television.

Hey team, moral leadership must drive business leadership which must drive governmental leadership. Mind control must start from somewhere special, where morals are made.

Now let's talk about gun control.

"Boundaries"

Boundaries are made to help us know what is our land and what is someone else's. There is usually a fence along the boundary of the property which clearly shows all where your land is. Out west there is barbed wire, on borders tall fences.

Sometimes boundaries are rivers or oceans. Countries are so defined.

Then again in some wildernesses or deserts there are no fences and the boundary is not visible. Now you don't want to cross over the border boundaries of some countries like North Korea or Iran for fear you might just go right to jail. Pain included.

In another sense, age can be a boundary or a limit to what one can do. Intelligence can be a boundary as ignorance can limit one's journey. Race can be a boundary as it limited movement in our past. Religion sets all kinds of limits that people can either follow or ignore. Much to talk about.

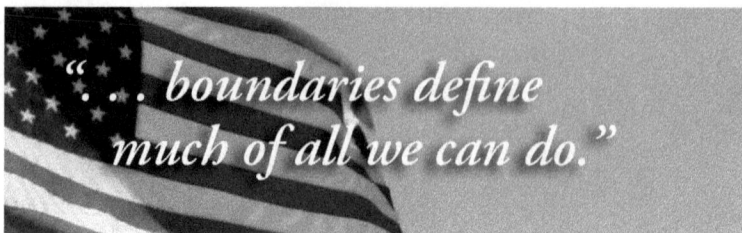

> *"... boundaries define much of all we can do."*

Regardless, boundaries define much of all we can do. If we choose to ignore them then someone will charge us with trespassing and criminal behavior. If we don't have the better lawyer we can end up in a small room with bars on the window and crummy food... and even torture...

So boundaries are important. Yes???

But then nobody, much less young people, wants someone else telling him what to do or where not to go.

So who respects boundaries these days???

There certainly are no moral boundaries anymore. All you have to do is click the box saying you are over 18 and there are no boundaries. Or click the box Parental Supervision Recommended and wooosh... all boundaries disappear and your fantasies are in high definition.

What about language? There are so many new words that are not yet in the dictionary that we can talk without boundaries or respect for others, much less ourselves.

Now we ask and allow our government to redefine our boundaries all the time. They love to do it. The politics of legislation. Moreover, we want them to do it! Then blame can be meted out to all those who do not respect the regulations, laws, and ordinances. We don't have to worry about what is right or wrong. It is already codified or written into law.

However, with so many laws it is no longer easy to discern boundaries. We need lawyers to help us. Fine print protects all but us. Voice prompts keep us from crossing communication boundaries. Where are we?

I have come across a fantastic Cuban family where all they know is boundaries and discipline. Where "NO" was the operative word, not "Yes."

Work ethic, respect, quality behavior, abnormal intelligence, and logic abound in their sons. Punishment was the reward for trespass.

This family has their next generation prepared for reality not fantasy. To me they are the new American model.

Boundaries are great. The right ones.

If we wish to be great again we might try to get back to those oldest 10 boundaries… They are in the No.1 best-selling book of all times.

Click and you can download it.

"Obvious"

Why is the obvious so unobvious to so many? Why is logic so difficult to understand?

Hey, let's go right to Washington for fun. We all postulate out here in the hinterlands that Washington just doesn't get it.

We work hard for a living and to hopefully pay our bills which will allow us to enjoy some things and help a few folks. We like to spend some time with our family and friends, enjoy a meal, and enjoy the sunrise and sunset. Work hard and feel good about yourself. Do good and feel good. Be honest and tell the truth. Then trust can facilitate growth and security. Simple.

We don't need more rules and more of those who regulate them. I thought government was to make our lives more simple and fruitful. And... protect our freedoms. But they seem to be on a Mission Impossible, to make our lives more impossible. What seems obvious to us out here in our

towns, businesses and churches is not on their screens and databases. Is it logical that they don't see our logic? KISS. Keep It Simple Senators.

Is it not obvious that no American can properly fill out their income tax form? Should not the tax system be done away with and replaced with a few flat tax codes? Does IRS stand for Intricate Revenue Stupification? What is the obvious?

Isn't it obvious that speeding is speeding?

Isn't it obvious that debt is debt?

Isn't it obvious that killing is murder?

Isn't it obvious that you go to a doctor if sick, not a lawyer?

Isn't it obvious that a family is a family?

Isn't it obvious that a church is for worship?

Isn't it obvious that evil is not good?

Isn't it obvious that common sense is being ignored?

The obvious has become humor of the bureaucrat. The new obvious is "the essential structuring and parsing of all definitions after vetting by legal."

I am keeping this short as it is obvious that the obvious is not high in the polls and that the upcoming mid-term elections will make it moot anyway.

"One-on-One"

The final solution. The other name for this piece. If you have made it this far and read all the "writs" up to this one then you are authorized to proceed.

I just googled the population of planet Earth. Right now it is 7,066,027,788. The population of the United States is 315,323,953. By the time you read this these numbers will be larger. Please make adjustments. We represent only 4% of the world's population, yet the largest economy, depending where China is today…around 1,341,403,687 or 19%… It would be fun to break it further down by race and religion… but I'll leave that up to you.

So statistically the world is growing rapidly in spite… economies are shifting… American pre-eminence is being challenged on all quarters. The destructive forces of the world have not been corralled. The Middle East is a nightmare boding future conflict and loss, as are other parts of the world. Are we no better off since the two world wars???

> ## "We all must start to be leaders one-on-one."

We appear to have turned our backs on much of our tradition. Some would say we have done the same with our Constitution as we parse it to suit contemporary correctnesses. Our citizens in our heartland are wary and not encouraged by government's ability to discipline itself and provide for the future. Something is amiss if one is honest. Polarization, the cancer of sensitivities, the abandonment of principles, the primacy of self, and the consensus of political correctness are defining our backbone. The curve is to the left.

It is becoming apparent we are not being ennobled by the masses. It is time for the individual to carve out his path and get on with getting on. It is time for him to stand for what he believes deep within and no longer waver to the loud voices in opposition. Protect your family, protect your town, protect your nation.

This is a call to change minds and hearts. To once more hold the damaged and give them hope. Not hope from new promises and laws, but hope from the arms of the neighbor who says, "No more." We are all neighbors. We have become islands unto ourselves, withdrawing from the cacophony of moral and spiritual decay. Where is the wronged to turn? The chilling wall of the voice prompt? The clinical charm of the online screen? No, the only solution is one-on-one. We all must start to be leaders one-on-one. Forget the big programs and their shallow promises. We must go from neighbor to neighbor, embracing and reassuring, embracing and reassuring. Over and over. But to do so we must have something to believe in.

Without God there is nothing, just a self-centered abyss. Anyway, that is my take on it all. Skeptics and atheists will scream, "Wrong," but I don't care anymore. I believe. Too Bad. Too Bad twenty times if that bothers you. I am going to attack my world one person at a time with love and laughter. One-on-one. Help one person at a time however much that person will accept and then move on, and move on again. I am here to serve not to take. Let me serve you.

"The Drill Instructor"

The Drill Instructor (DI) barks out his commands to the frightened cadre. "Gimme 50!!!" "Backs straight!!!" "Chest must touch ground!!!" "Full extension!!!" "Get that back straight, how many times do I have to tell you?!!!" "OK, stay at lean and rest until I come back, children!"

Do you think they make Marines, soldiers, much less SEALs by asking them what they would prefer to do? Do you think the Drill Instructors have graduated from sensitivity training? Are Democratic Constitutional rights in effect? Are the recruits entitled?

I postulate that this just must might be about life and death, not feelings. I think this may be about protecting your freedoms and right to complain. But this cannot happen without young men prepared for battle and for death. Huuuhhh??? Hello?? You have got to be kidding? OMG you can't be serious? Death doesn't happen other than on the news and usually far away. Whatever. Text me later...I am busy.

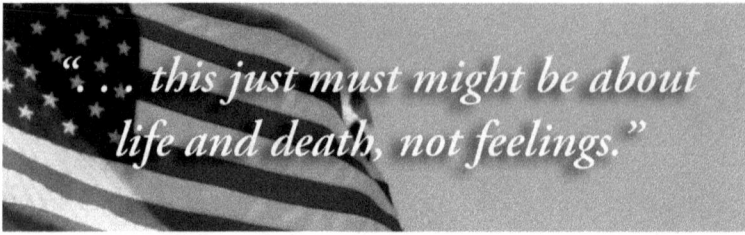

> *"... this just must might be about life and death, not feelings."*

I am of the opinion that every young able-bodied male should be drafted. Boys become men much sooner than on the playing fields or the streets.

We sure don't like systems which tell us what to do. It is like it is in our DNA to rebel against authority. Go away Dad, go away teacher, go away policeman, go away boss, go away reality. I am armored with my self-serving iPhone and the courage of my social network.

We allow the Drill Instructors of life to make us miserable as long as it keeps us from getting killed. We love our bodies as they are our ego cathedrals.

But what about the Drill Instructor in the clouds? He wants to save our souls and enrich our lives beyond our wildest imagination. Problem is... we don't have any imagination.

How many individuals choose paths right into the combat zones of greed, lust, envy, pride, gluttony, anger, and filth? Drugs, alcohol, sex, vanity, indifference, and jealousy and... on and on. "Well, I didn't think it would be this bad. A little more won't hurt…" Consciences trampled by disdain for authority and logic. Where is the Drill Instructor when I need him? Everyone doesn't screw up their lives. I see some happy people around… No not the hypocrites… just a lot of normal people going about their business, helping others, and laughing. How do I become one of them?

Well, duuuhhh??? Hello, The Drill Instructor in the sky!

No pain no gain they always said…

"Looking Down"

Looking down on someone has always been kind of snobby. When you are young and understand relatively little (different these days, of course) you have many opinions of others shaped by other's opinions. "She thinks she is so important," etc., you know... People are looked down upon because of pseudo social status, taste, background, intelligence, looks, thinking... Have not every one of us been guilty of looking down on someone once in our lives? Or on the celebrity who has finally fallen???

Fighter pilots look down when they are going to bomb someone. Divers look down when approaching a wreck. Politicians look down on us when they disregard our opinions. Muslims look down on Christians.

As you get older you finally learn that looking down is arrogant and ultimately creates problems that come back to haunt us big time. Am I better than you because I can pick out your flaw?

"We are becoming a Looking Down culture."

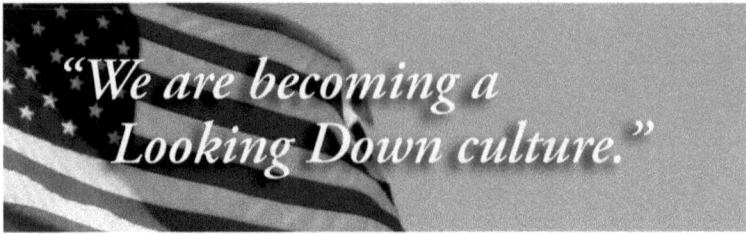

I'll bet that the new social networks are infused with small talk about every single person encountered. I'll bet every iPhone has texted some criticism of some other person. Looking down on them. And it is absolutely hilarious that all heads are looking down as they are walking and texting. We are the biggest cartoon ever!!! Go into a restaurant these days and everyone is looking down at their cell phones, not the menu!!! And the kids??? Forget it.

We are becoming a Looking Down culture. We are looking down on ourselves. We can't see where we are going because we are looking down.

Pretty soon postures will change and we will no longer be able to look Up where the answers are.

"Evolution"

Can't anyone prove anything? We are so wound up, liberal and conservative, with issues of rights and interpretations and political correctness that we are self-destructing in a mush of counter-counter-accusations. Are we evolving into intellectual extinction???

It used to be that we believed in our cornerstones. Our emigrant forefathers came here with solid dreams and beliefs. They adjusted to the English language and the porridge of cultures that became America. They fought rotten wars with courage and pride. They gave up limbs and psyche to protect our way of life… And our Constitution.

Where are we? Has sacrifice been in vain? Where are we going? Tell me!!! Someone tell me!!! No. More importantly, where did we come from??? Where???

The atheist believes in evolution and science can take us back thousands of years. It is fascinating stuff and our

DNA appears to be rich with all kinds of primate and sub-primate ancestors. (I know, I have often been accused of thinking like a monkey by my wife… and we won't quote the other things she has compared me to…) OK, and when the astronomers look deep into the heavens at the current record holder for farthest galaxy away, MACS0647-JD, a trifle 13.3 billion light-years away, they cannot conclude that this is the last galaxy. You and I know the odds are that if we got a better telescope the end would never be in sight. So existence seems to go out to infinity and beyond. Go figure? Does that make sense? Balderdash. Of course, this is just this one man's opinion.

Oh, I forgot the Big Bang Theory. That is even more ridiculous. What started that?? The NRA??

The renowned scientist atheists, Keith, Watson, Moore and Epp, said that they just could not prove evolution. Science could not prove ultimate evolution. That that whole rationale was defective, reaching a dead end in supposition. But because they chose not to believe in creation or God, they had no choice but to support evolution. LOOK AT THESE QUOTES from a SEAL buddy's paper*.

Sir Arthur Keith states "Evolution is unproved and improvable; we believe it only because the only alternative is special creation which is unthinkable."

Professor D.M.S. Watson expresses, "Evolution itself is accepted by zoologists, not because it has been observed to occur or can be proven by logically coherent evidence, but because the only alternative, special creation, is clearly unthinkable."

Professor T.L. Moore states, "The more one studies paleoanthropology, (the fossil record), the more certain one becomes that evolution is based on faith alone."

Theodore H. Epp remarked that everything we can see exists, but since we refuse to believe in God, we choose to believe that it was brought to existence through evolution. Epp goes on to say that you cannot believe in God, and not give him credit for your creation.

It takes a greater leap of faith to believe in evolution than it does in God. Mock me all you want. Bring it on. Love it.

How in the world has the Bible helped so many for so long? How does its words resonate so clearly from some pretty rough and uneducated guys 2,000 years ago? That

---

* Quotes taken from the Paper: Creation/Evolution, (THE BURIED TRUTHS), by Rey Ruidiaz

makes no sense unless it does. What is wrong with right? What is good about evil? The Bible may be stories to the atheist, to the cynic, but to beautiful people I know it is a tool for clarity and purpose, for humility and unselfishness, for giving and not taking, for serving and not being served. Lives have been saved by Faith, lives have been turned around by Faith, even death has been ennobled by Faith.

I cannot see galaxies, but I can see need. And we need God.

Creation is all that makes sense.

"Please Pass This On"

I don't know about the rest of you, but I delete all "please pass it on's." Maybe it stems from being a kid once when everyone was telling you what to do? Maybe it comes from being an adult and having to consider what others' opinions are ad nauseum? One used to pass things of merit on to friends so we could all profit from the wisdom of experience... Or something like that...

Now that we are blessed with the internet and social media up the gazoo everybody is sending these inane observations about politics, religion, social injustice, and marginal humor with the caveat, "please pass this on". If you have to say "Please pass this on," then that is an immediate red light to the diminished worth of the suggestion and content. Delete immediately or you run the risk of diminishing your credibility. Quality should stand on its own. Today the slightest quality of something is so embellished and over promoted that we can no longer discern quality. Stand back and look at the world and our morphing cultures. Qualities

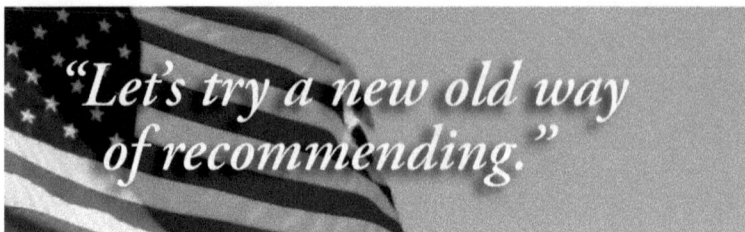

"Let's try a new old way of recommending."

are obscured by trumped up validation and endorsement. Values which represent the quality assets of life are obscured by criticism and dismissive humor.

Maybe if you pay more for something you can be assured of quality. No… better wait for the discounted price to establish quality… Pass it on.

Let's try a new old way of recommending. Show me first. Partner in truth… one person at a time.

Stand for quality and do not deflect responsibility.

Never pass anything on until you delete the "Please pass this on" tag.

Make life better by standing your ground.

Please pass this on…

"The Decision"

Life isn't fair. Some are lucky and some are not. Some are born in the United States and some are born in Africa. Some are born into Christianity and some are born into Islam. Some live their lives in Nikes and some in bare feet. Some should be glad and some should be angry. Some have iPads and some have nothing. Some travel and some go nowhere. Some are rich and some are poor. Why are there slums?

We send our sons to fight wars to protect our shores. It has to be done… or you have your head in the sand or in your social network looking down. In the military these sons bond intensely in ways we do not know. It is the finest of wines. It is idealism in the raw. When a life is lost it is like a baby being ripped from a womb. Multiple combat tours with the same unit forges courage and knowledge in an intimacy that is foreign to most. Living the extremes of trust.

> ## "The new combat is with the bureaucracies."

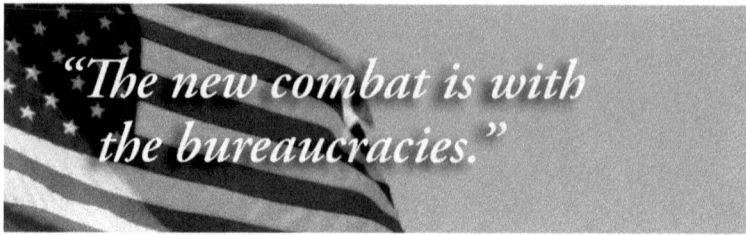

IED's (Improvised Explosive Devices) have made it all the more absurd and difficult for the participants. Lost limbs and lives in an instant. The victim who lives is almost worse off. Sent home. No more responsibility for his buddies. A nightmare of pretense and bad dreams lies ahead.

Veterans don't talk about what they saw as we would not understand, much less appreciate. So the silent prison forms. Peers are no longer that. Jobs are very difficult to find. The new combat is with the bureaucracies. Self lost in the mountain of forms and databases. No one hires. Interviews are fewer and less comfortable. Pride diminished. A life feels lost.

Why are veteran suicides greater than combat deaths?

There should be a quota for all businesses to hire veterans. They put it all on the line for us. Why can't we for them?

Let's take their tragic decision away from them.

"Drones"

Is there a place for social media (SM) in combat? Facebook, Skype, Viber and texting are a few of the new psyche-defining influences on the spontaneous thinking and decision making capabilities of our youth and future soldiers. Do you see a young person anymore without a cell phone in their hands or their ear buds in their ears? This is a cultural and ego defining new paradigm.

Forward to the next ground war in the Middle East or wherever. Do the Sergeants confiscate all cell phones upon enlisting? Is the soldier's next break a reassuring text to someone??? How dependent are we becoming on SM?

I say thank God for the drones. They are allowing the foot soldier to relax until the danger is mapped or taken care of by the drones. Whew, they have time to take a picture and text it. And… feel a little more comfortable… Put ring tone on mute. In combat, all ring tones must be on mute… It can still yield the reassuring vibration when the girlfriend or drinking buddy is calling…

"I say thank God for the drones."

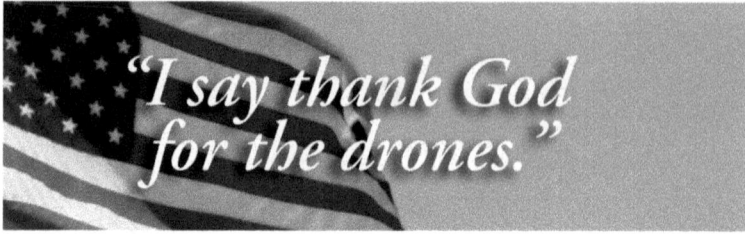

Back in the States at Drone Command Central, the drone pilot can watch his console and sneak a few texts in. Being a drone pilot can be boring as drones repeat themselves a lot and fly in circles... but it is a good job and it allows more time for everyone to SM and sustain propped up identities that have been nurtured in cyberspace.

I hope they don't outlaw domestic drones. Enough is enough. Leave our drones alone. It will be reassuring to know they are up there protecting us. Very targeted invasions of privacy and data capture are OK. It is the fact that they will multiply fast like buzzing locusts as businesses and bureaucracies map our SM habits to determine if we have any individuals remaining. But I am sure Washington can regulate and protect our rights with the new DRA (Drone Regulation Agency).

Drones will be able to detect large metal objects like guns and track them while checking registration tags that will be imbedded in each. Unregistered guns on felons will be disabled by laser. Keep the drones, as I am really reversing my feelings towards them. Of course, they must be registered and vetted by the DRA.

Maybe there is a Heaven after all. All you have to do now is text a good friend to get reassurance that you are liked. Cyber angels. Pharmaceutical companies will lose fortunes as the markets for happy pills dry up.

We are just beginning to grasp the full potential of drones. This is new territory just like when our settlers pushed west and discovered Los Angeles.

"FBF"

I know that it is really time to be positive. Nothing ever gets accomplished with a negative predisposition. Everyone makes mistakes. Things are done that are regrettable.

I hate to say it but we all have done some very wrong things that have hurt or disappointed another person. Lies have been told that created ripple effects way beyond intended. Deeds perpetrated in selfishness leaving deep scars on the victim. Lives have been stopped in their tracks by evil and selfishness. Angers are festering deep within souls with no easy way out other than the dead end streets of drugs and alcohol.

Unintended consequences. Hmmm… much to ponder in our own lives. I wish technology could invent a drone that could locate those in distress and zap them with joy. Or better yet… zap them with forgiveness.

You see, the only cure for hurt and blame is forgiveness. Angers are carried and stifle growth, reconciliation, and

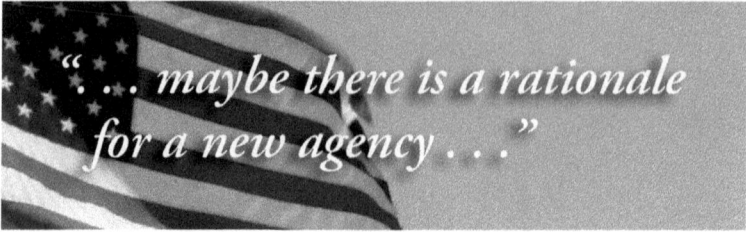

hope. Some keep angers to their graves from generations ago. A total waste of life and potential. How to unburden? Therapy works to a certain degree. It starts the journey. But without forgiveness and the courage to forgive the hurt lives on as personal demons. Demons.

Why is man so embroiled in bitterness? Because he can't forgive... I know this is preposterous with all the unthinkable evil that has destroyed millions of lives. But... anybody got a better idea?

Wait... as new governments are revealing their infinite capability to manage anything that is based on data... maybe there is a rationale for a new agency, the FBF or Federal Bureau of Forgiveness. Types of pain and evil can be classified, quantified, indexed, and codified so appropriate certificates of forgiveness can be granted. The applicant lines will be long at first, but eventually they will thin out as relief is achieved. There will be corporate contracts to assist, but not without full government oversight. More federal employment will be a collateral economic boost.

This all about identifying problems and solutions that can be managed efficiently by forward thinking. The solution is the forgiveness revolution.

You don't have to die on a Cross to provide forgiveness. Or do you?

"27,000 Pages"

When I was a kid, things were pretty simple. If Johnny said something mean to me I just hit him and that was the end of it. I then grew a bit and got my Kentucky driver's license, signed one form, drove the test... and was free for life! There was a thing called the handshake back then. It worked for most agreements. I wasn't old enough for a job or taxes. Life was easy to understand. There weren't many lawyers.

I went in the Navy and my income tax form was really simple as pie. You could figure it out... maybe two to three pages, a deduction, and you got a check. This worked for a long time. I got out and it still was a non-event. Your company supplied your W-2, you deducted your mortgage stuff, some charity, and put a stamp on the envelope. It was a little more for a small business, but the accountant had it figured out. Fast forward. Today's tax code is 27,000 pages. The fine print tries to outwit the payee. Every possible interpretation is potentially covered in infinite

"Who writes this stuff anyway?"

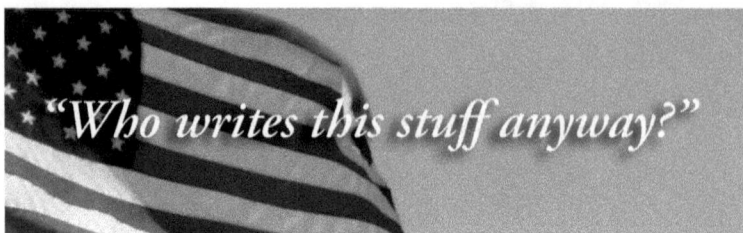

fine print. Hello??? Tilt!!! How did this happen? Who is to blame? This is evil. This is bureaucracy gone wild. Where is the Bureaucracy Police? Where is transparency? It has been stabbed in the aorta by keyboards and fine print. Is this really government protecting us or is it white collar crime on the grandest scale? Where are the environmental watchdogs? This is our economic environment that is being strangled by an administrative shell game.

Who writes this stuff anyway? Who signs off on it? Isn't it time to say "Throw the bums in jail!"? Every government says they are going to make things simple and they lie to us. Remember the 9-9-9 concept? It may have been brilliant with a few adjustments, but NOT 27,000 pages worth!!!

We need SEAL politicians who will not quit or flinch in the face of fully armed special interest attorneys. It is time to "just do it." Chuck it all.

And now that we have a concept... How about applying it to the deficit? The budget. The entitlements. Make a bill a bill with no attachments, no pork, no special interest addendums. Make everything stand on its own. Just do it.

Well, maybe this postulating is too late. Maybe 27,000 pages has sealed our fate and the cliff is here. I see the top of the waterfall 100 yards ahead... The noise... aghhh... See ya. Hooyah.

"The Mother Lode"

In the mid 1800's in the Sierra Nevada of California there was an enormous migration of entrepreneurs with picks and shovels racing to find eternal happiness and security in the wealth of a giant vein of gold in the hills. And the California Gold Rush was on. Tents became towns. The scream of "Eureka!" became a new word in our vocabulary, resonating around the world. It was as if all problems would be solved. Money was the root of all peace, not evil. Or that was what one believed, what one hoped, what one had faith in.

Life was not easy in those days. No phones. No computers. No movies. No TV. Just guns and whiskey.

Fighting broke out. Fortunes were stolen. It was the wild west. No laws. No regulations. No codes. No taxman. No 27,000 page tax code. No lawyers. No media.

Hope turned to tragedy as the latecomers piled into the instant cities. Evil became good or vice versa. This mother lode became temporal. But if you stand back...look at the power it had.

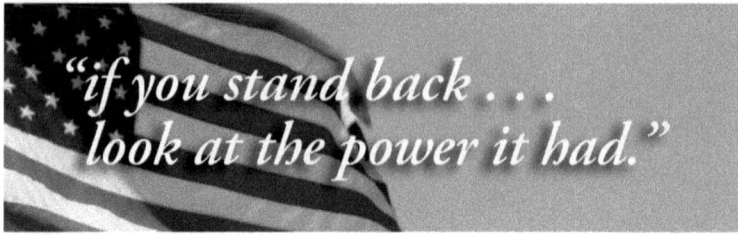

Tens of thousands came from Latin America, Europe, and China. San Francisco grew from 200 residents in 1846 to 36,000 in 1852. Billions of dollars of gold was amassed by a few. Most went home with what they started with. Railroads were built. Claims were staked. 100,000 native Indians died… 4,500 murdered.

The Mother Lode was the mother of much pain.

False hopes? Dead end streets? Rumor-driven expectations of fulfillment?

There are all kinds of other Mother Lodes in life, all promising happiness and relief from pain. There are the excesses of drugs and alcohol. There the joys of sex beckoning destruction. There is the distraction of self. There is the trap of social media. Our new world is full of disguised answers to nowhere.

How did we get this far? Hopes dashed. Endless conflict. Endless arguing. Endless war.

There remains the Mother Lode everyone searches for after all others have failed. But we are so stubborn. We are so sure of ourselves. We are so unable to give up our sense of self. We are so unable to take advice. Over and over we fight our innate call to good. We cannot look around and take heed from what is strong, from what is right, from what is unselfish. The thought of being willing to give up control is abhorrent. Don't tread on me. Don't tell me what to do. Then why do we go to school but to learn? To be told what to do? Why do we accept training? Why does a gun require training to not abuse? Why does a child need forceful direction?

Why do we turn away from words like values and truth as if they were ultra conservative radical affronts? Who defines what these days? Is truth only in legislation? Are we not capable of standing for the simplicity of moral courage and sacrifice? Can we not applaud the soldier of war and of values? What does the farmer say to his son? "Listen to me, son. Work hard every day. Protect your family. Do not sin. Always tell the truth. Show respect to others. Be humble. Embrace forgiveness. Love your mom. Do these and you are my son."

The Mother Lode today is a return to the values that made us strong and unique. To our Constitution and our Bible. The Mother Lode is the Cross.

"What Can I Do For You?"

Nothing. I don't want you to do anything. You don't know what I am going through. You don't know what I am feeling. If I am bleeding and you can see the blood you can help. Get a Band-Aid, apply a tourniquet, raise my head, give me a Heimlich, call 911. Your eyes tell you the obvious and you can help.

In the majesty of our unique creation we celebrate and reject our uniqueness. We are really shy and don't want to admit all that we have to admit. More importantly we don't want to forgive when the pain is ours to manage and bear. Anger replaces acceptance. Forgiveness becomes demeaning to our self.

But without forgiveness we cease to exist outside of a world of pain. How long we choose to carry pain and hurt is our decision, even if it drags others into the despair. Too bad. Anger fuels perseverance.

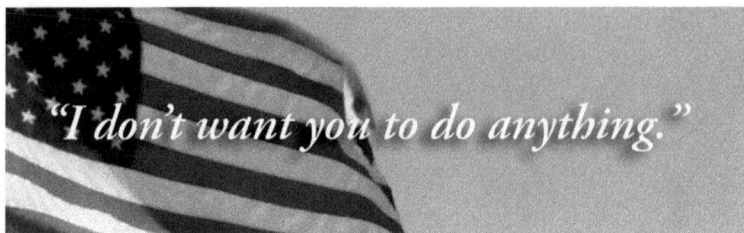
"*I don't want you to do anything.*"

I cannot be free until I forgive. I try every other possible angle… but it still comes back to forgiveness. If I refuse to forgive, or give it lip service I am owned by a weight of my own choosing. This darkens the air around all near me, friends and family alike.

OK… Really? Ok… how do I forgive? How do I try it? Can I take it back??? Well… you can take it back, but then you haven't forgiven… and back to square one.

Ok, I forgive you, I really do. If I do… Hey I don't feel as bad… Can't be for real?

They say, "Try it, you'll like it." Maybe that person I still don't like… always bothers me… glad he is not around… yep… wish he would go away. But… the only way he can really go away is if I make him go away by forgiveness… then he leaves my mind…

We were all forgiven once. But most don't want to admit or even think about this. We want to be us and not have to give up any control.

What can I do for you? Forgive me for not being more understanding... Just do anything. Even pray.

At least it wasn't me on the Cross...

"The New Old Narcotic"

Narcotics cover a myriad of drugs. There are the hard drugs, there are the smoking kind, and there are those hidden in prescriptions. You pay a lot of money or you pay a little, but we all know you pay… and pay in currencies of lost lives and pain. Yep, the drug war is beyond our comprehension. We talk like we understand it… but we have no clue until it hits us… Why is your first hit usually free?? Because the seller knows the false euphoria is the worm on his cash hood. Adios life, hola dreamsville. We all believe the dream under the influence, the feeling of well-being, the crooked smile of contentment is the answer to everything, especially self-doubt.Nirvana is within reach. Heaven is a myth as you feel it in the now. Life is not easy. No one is entitled to anything but hard work and honesty and truth and its rewards. Why do we think life is supposed to be easy? Why do we think there are short-cuts to happiness??? Why? Please ask yourself why? Who sold us this illusion? Movies? Television? Advertising? Who? Why did we buy into it so readily?

> *"There is no known recovery program with a cure."*

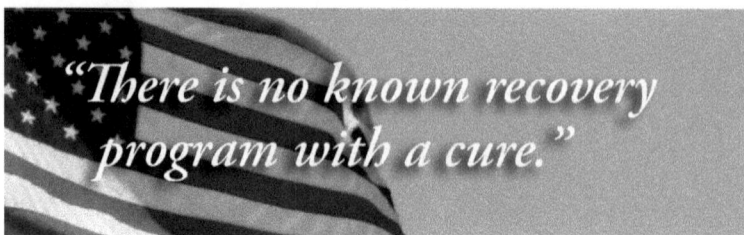

Feeling good and the desire to feel good is its own addiction. We are offered so many ways to achieve it… and most all are deceivingly worthless… and we find out too late. We ignore the advice of the knowledgeable and look the other way as we sense the stimulant taking effect. Alcohol works well too. Any excess works. Why do we chase addictions? Insecurity? Self-image worries? Hiding from the scrutiny or opinion of others?

Then there is the Attention Addiction. Why do we revere celebrities? Because we love the idea of all the attention they get. Simple. But, boy are we hooked… Red carpet hooked. And we have these elaborate award ceremonies to further celebrate the attention of the attention gods.

Doesn't each one of us like a little attention? Some are shy and don't… and some feign shyness and love attention. Most of us just love attention. Until now we had to earn it. That is, until now. I repeat… Until now we had to earn it. That is, until now.

We are at the dawn of the newest and oldest and most powerful narcotic of all… SELF. The drug has been formulated. There is no known recovery program with a cure. This attention deficit disorder has become an Attention Addiction enabled by the infinite access provided by Social Media. Every moment we have a self doubt it can be erased by texting someone who likes us or will say something nice. Every instant we feel a little down, social media will provide the narcotic of superficial affection and acknowledgement. Why are heads lowered everywhere you go? Because they are being relieved by the assurances from social networking. Look around. See the narcotic. Happiness is now found in looking down.

No longer by looking up where the real answers lie.

"War"

"War is an ugly thing, but not the ugliest of things. The decayed and degraded state of moral and patriotic feeling which thinks that nothing is worth war is much worse..." (John Stuart Mill).

I have never used a quote before... but I just finished an intense book by a SEAL, "Damn Few." This jumped out at me so strong as it is themed throughout all my writs. So let's explore it a little... And see if we can reject the premise.

As we all know war is repugnant because of all the innocent people that suffer horribly from wounds and displacement, much less death. Idiotic regimes, egos, and cultures espouse freedom and compassion for their poor only to subjugate them to false cultures of corruption. While, at the same time, demonizing our liberties and success. With our great intellects we dismiss their posturing as just illusions of danger. We analyze and yield responsibility to the talking

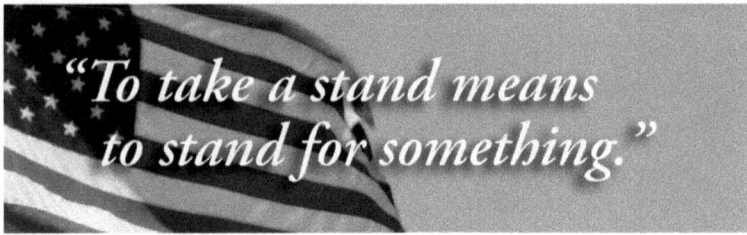

heads and pundits in the media. They are all over perspective, truth, and the infinite postulations of politicians. They are more right than we are. We allow them to be… and we become complicit in the advent of war.

I have never seen a body blown to bits or a child with a bullet hole in her head. Do I need to see that to take a stand? Do I need to turn off the TV and do something? Can I stop a bullet coming for some child's brain?

We all have to answer that question. We all have to think about it and take a stand. Not to is to be a coward and an irresponsible adult who chooses to facilitate evil. That's how I call it.

To take a stand means to stand for something. Where is the line you draw? Does anything have value? Define values. Whatever made this country great? Or when did you think it might have been great?

We are a good people. We are a blessed people. We have a great Constitution and a great history of compassion. Is this worth protection? Do we realize we are on an invisible slippery slope to losing it all? There is a moral decay in our country that is almost systemic. Laws are reducing responsibility. Behavior is being redefined to permit anything under the umbrella of rights. Sin now has rights. Christians are now being marginalized. Showing the flag is now problematic. Labels have proliferated such that anything good is easily categorized as bad. It is so subtle. It is so deadly. Our internal bickering and blaming is eroding our society. The rest of the world sees it as weakness and the forces of war are being emboldened.

We will be at war again. It may be this year… or next… but it is inevitable the way we are behaving.

"Nothing is worth war" is becoming our motto. We are actually saying that we will not fight. We will talk and threaten while our economy and our military erode. Paper tiger.

Our children aren't worth war?

If you touch my car I will kill you.

"Similarities"

Similarities. We are in awe of similarities. We share similarities with other humans and even living things. Crazy. How can one be so different and yet find a similarity elsewhere? We can easily find similarities with our parents. Heck our DNAs are similar. Dolphins are mammals, so are we. They are magical as we superimpose feelings and responses on them… Fascinating. Ever swum with one??? Kindred spirits. Why?

Of course there are the monkeys and all warm blooded creatures that breathe air. But we will just stick with our fellow humans for today. I don't get intelligent thought. How could things have been written and discovered thousands of years ago, way before any communication systems, much less electricity? Amazing. History is amazing. They were bloody and fought a lot back then. Has it changed that much??? It's just different. They fought to protect family and values way back then, however crude. Their truths were similar to ours… Maybe less perverted by sentiment and media… maybe..?

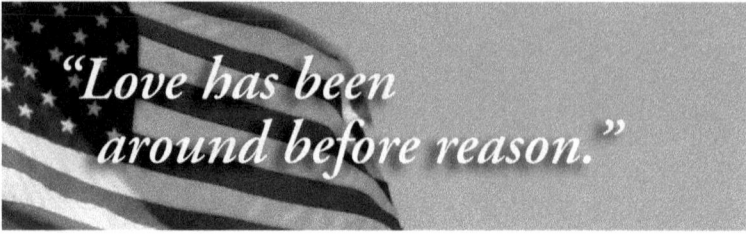

Love has been around before reason. Couldn't have had kids without some sensations of affection and caring. Even caveman and cavewoman. Think about it… We had to get here from somewhere. Forget the ape stuff and celestial God particles… let's stay real.

Of course if one gazes millions of light years into the farther galaxies you can find similarities… Certainly beauty. But then again we can look at sunsets on the ocean… each unique, but always similarities… We can criticize with similarities or praise with comparisons. We like to have someone say we look like some celebrity. Plastic surgery is available to the vain who wish, in the back of their minds, to look like someone else.

Then again there are our heroes. False and real. Why would one not wish to have similarities to a Lincoln, a Martin Luther King, or a gifted person we may have been exposed to? Not one of any we pick are without flaws. None without sin. But it is the humans that we have to choose from. "I would like to be like…" We have all said that. But maybe not if you had walked in their shoes. Maybe not if you knew their upbringing or secret pains.

This similarity thing gets complicated real fast. Heaven forbid one has similarities to a tragic or evil person. I want similarities to a good person, an unselfish person, a humble person, a successful person. I was lucky... that was my dad. But now we have to worry did we live up to them? Did we make them proud? Or, on the contrary, if your parent wasn't so good, or even never showed up… you still want to make them proud in spite of their failings. You also want to find forgiveness for them so the pain chain is broken and their heritage can no longer hurt anyone. This is complicated terrain. From childhood, deep in our sensitivities and identity, lie questions, insecurities, and self-doubt. We need to find similarities with the strong and virtuous to embolden ourselves into noble and joyful pursuits. We need to be similar to or synonymous with values. We need to be known for values. We need to "hang" with people of values.

But not on a Cross.

"The Call"

The Call. When will that call come? Aren't we all waiting for that call that will unlock some secret pain from the past? Is not every person carrying some feeling from their past that is unresolved?

Life is about processing all the joyful and painful experiences that come one's way. No person is without sin. Many try to pretend that sin is too strong a label for their sensitivities or philosophy. We want our sins to just go away and never be heard from again. Or the word is stupid and does not exist... The funny thing, I mean really funny, is that we are being dishonest with ourselves. The memory of sins never goes away. It never fades away. For if sin is not dealt with head on it will continue to coexist with our façade. It takes courage to be honest with oneself. Real courage.

There are the hurts of others that we also carry deep within. Hurts others have done to us. Hurts that we assume,

accept, and carry. Is not every one of us angry at someone? Anger eats so insidiously at us. We don't know how to deal with it. Some just try to ignore. Some pray. No solution works other than forgiveness. You cannot be free from the hurt or anger until you forgive. It is the most powerful tool we have, but it takes humility and courage to make it happen. Do you know how many years can go by with hidden hurts weighing us down? We are stubborn about trying every other approach but forgiveness. Even drugs or alcohol or addictions cannot work…

Courage comes from conscience and grace. Courage comes from goodness. Courage comes from caring beyond self. Without courage there is little hope. The way out of difficult times is courage. That is what Medals of Honor are about. Each of us is capable of forgiveness. Each of us can achieve our own invisible Medal of Honor.

The call. Make the call to that person you need to ask forgiveness from. Make that call to forgive that person.

Courage? You bet. Without forgiveness life has little chance. Without forgiveness you have little chance.

If the call comes you also have to be able to receive it. The courage on the other end must be embraced with courage and humility. The effort must be acknowledged. There is no other rational choice. Love.

I received that call today. Out of the damn blue. No idea what courage it took for my caller to make it. Both in tears. I still feel the courage. I still choke up. She too.

The power of forgiveness explodes its intensity in love and grace. Words are fleeting to describe. Who to thank? Who would know what this means but the caller and the called.

Without the example on the Cross we would not make the call.

"Calendar"

The Calendar is the most ubiquitous organizer. Everyone uses it. Every bank in the world must yield to our calendar. Think about all the planning that goes on from January to December that we depend on. Birthdays, appointments, meetings, weddings, parties, and funerals... think how intertwined we all are with our calendars... on refrigerators, garage walls, school classrooms... even missile silos and coffee shops in Tehran... You name it our calendar is everywhere!!!

New Year's Day is January 1 and we start anew. Although December 31 was no different... January 1 is a holiday and we all get to watch football games and try to forget the night before. Holidays are special days all year long reminding us of special people and ideas to commemorate. Today we have calendars on our computers and phones and iPads that highlight, detail, and recur all kinds of events and notes. Amazing. Truly amazing.

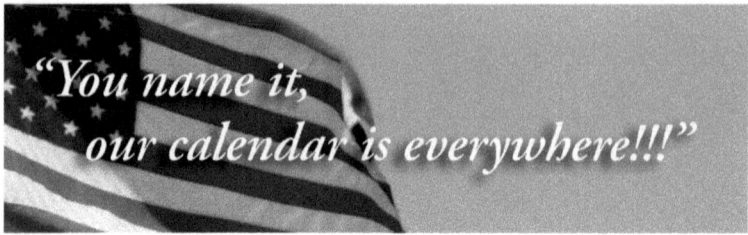

Well, now we are well into the year 2013. We know what happened in 1940, we know what happened in 1865, 1776, 1492, 1310, 899, 562, 243, 102, 36 and 01. With modern technology and Wikipedia most all history is at our fingertips. All woven into our calendar.

Well I have a problem with this blatantly religious calendar. It is 2013 AD.

Why has the calendar been protested? Why has Christmas not been deleted?

In fact every month is incorrect. Every day is dictated by this religious document. We are hypocrites by selectively allowing some religious symbols to stand while others not. Crosses are banned from public places. So should be the calendar.

We should be more sensitive to the year as defined by non-Christians. In fact it would be secularly correct to ban our calendar as it imposes a Christian Anno Domini overlay on everything. B.C. means Before Christ. You mean things happened before Christ? Why does Christ have to define and organize so much of what we do?

Where are the protesters? Where is the ACLU? Why hasn't someone invented a more sensible calendar? It is time to respect the sensitivities of those who believe in nothing. What is Faith but fables perpetrated? In fact we get along just fine without it imposing hope and Truth on us.

We created our own existence when our ancestors got together for a big bang… or big bong… whatever.

All I need is my time clock. Oops… it has that darn 2013 year thing on it…

"Leave Me Alone"

Leave me alone. Why can't you just leave me alone? I can figure it out myself. I don't need anybody to help me… Acteth the 10 year old… sayeth the 15 year old… and sayeth the 21 year old… and sayeth the 30 year old… and sayeth the 50 year old… and thinketh the 60 year old…

If you never said or felt this then you are lying to yourself and all of us. What is it in our humble beings that makes us think we are the center of "rightness"? Why do we reject assistance other than training to drive a car or school or work training? But the personal, internal training is handled only by our self. Don't tell me what to do. Don't correct my perception. I can judge just fine on my own. I will let you know if I need your advice, my dear parent or friend. Don't worry… Like… I will call you when I am already in the hospital.

"I can figure it out myself."

These walls of defense and insecurity inhabit each and every one of us. Think about it. Some have already put this down as this is taboo territory. Don't go there. Don't tell anyone what to do. I am always right.

This a blindness of most all. We are our own judge and jury and we do not need counsel, aka a thought attorney. This is the ultimate arrogance of "me-centric" thinking. I am guilty. If my parents told me what to do I... "whatever." It is especially painful when your own children don't want you advising them of anything unless they ask. Which, of course, they never do. LOL.

OMG, this LMA (Leave Me Alone) syndrome is just getting worse... as so much time is now being taken away by the self-affirmation of Facebook and texting. DTMWTD (Don't Tell Me What To Do) is the new psychology until you need a psychiatrist. Then you just tell them everything you want and then ask to be left alone. Comical to say the least.

Is there Hope? Always. But it lies in listening. Not to your intellect, not to your phone, not to your libido, not to your feelings. But to your heart. If you can still find it, The Truth lies there…

Godspeed.

"Progress is Certain"

As we go down new-found roads there has to be a little time for humor. So bear with me. Do not judge or vilify. This is not meant to offend any human being other than some in the Middle East...

I really love my wife and I need to protect her from all future administrative bumps in the road. I don't know how the legal winds will blow after I am gone. But with all tradition now subject to intense scrutiny, parsing and repositioning I have to plan ahead. If you are found out to be a "traditionalist" then you will be re-categorized as a person of the new extreme. Being a conservative you are already marginalized. If you are a person of Faith? Forget it. You are labeled as rigid and archaic. Get with it people, this is the New World Order.

Who was it that said... "Give me Liberalism or give me death"???

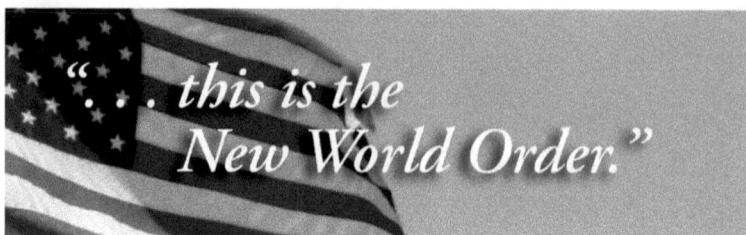

Anyway, back to protecting my wife. The new tax codes that have not been read or created will aptly reclassify her as needing reduced deductions as she will fall into the OSC coding. Opposite-Sex Ceremony? Fortunately we do not have kids… as the OSC Medicare expenses will be much higher for the father and mother due to the proven therapy assistance required to protect the children from the disharmonious and non-natural nurturing environment they will be subjected to by a male and female in constant disagreement.

Think of all the forms they will have to fill out to qualify for anything.

First thing to do tomorrow is to reapply our marriage certificate for an Opposite-Sex Marriage Certificate so we will be properly registered and scanned.

Oh well… progress is certain.

"Fear"

What is common about Boston? New York? Newtown? Aleppo? Kabul?

Evil and hate coexist with truth and love. Not to acknowledge either is to live in denial. Evil cannot just be legislated away which is the contemporary leaning. Evil is our enigma. Today we have a problem (or "issue") with confronting it. This is a very personal journey and decision. You either accept evil as a reality or not. To me there is no choice. And passivity in the face of evil courts harm to all including one's family. No has to mean "No." I am tired of the "maybe" and the parsing of truth.

As a nation we have to stand for something. Our Constitution is a good start.

Hello people. If we decide that evil is benign then there is no need for a military. Open the borders and embrace infinite diversity and give housing to all who hate us. Goodbye cathedral… Hello mosque. And goodbye English as an added bonus.

Minds can become demented when fed bigoted or hateful input. As they say… bad in bad out. The Boston desecration came from a demented mind fed with hate. A hate that was far from any truth and creating an evil energy inside a tortured ego searching for self-esteem.

Our world and media is full of easy access to every kind of thought and philosophy regardless of merit. Our institutions of morality are on the wane. Our self-enlightened freedom of thought is making us vulnerable. We are not strong because we do not believe any longer. We look for others' opinions to form our core thinking. Our media-enriched frontal lobes beg for more assurance from social media and texting.

We are entering a post-Christian era. The new rules are found in fine print, regulations, forms, and laws… and universal registration scanning or whatever.

The "why" of Boston will be very important. We will capture and kill. But will we find the right path to become strong again in spirit and soul?

If not, then fear will be our new bridesmaid.

"Born Into"

Wait a second. Wait… hold all that opinion and judgment.

Shoes are made for walking. Whose shoes have you walked in?

When you were born where was it? California, Uganda, Damascus, Port-au-Prince, or Pyongyang? How come I was born in New York? Sure glad I was not born in all those other places where discomfort and injustice is the rule. Do we ever really count our blessings before we judge all those souls fighting misery and corruption every hour of every day?

Don't get me wrong… right is not wrong… and wrong is not right. Meaning evil is not good… You get to choose how to lead your life…. You get to choose what is of value. But where you were born, through zero choice of your own, makes your chance to lead a good life a toss-up. If you live in a third world country your media access is a joke… or certainly the quality of it. Your freedom from want …

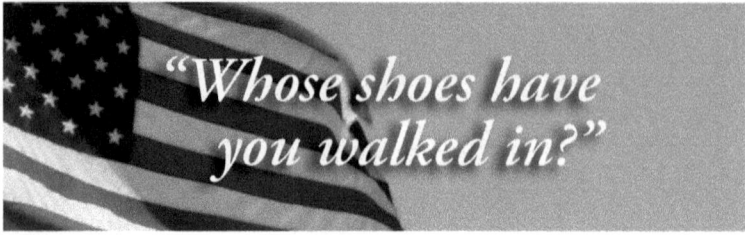

"Whose shoes have you walked in?"

both physical and mental… is marginal. How do you avoid bad political teachings? How do you avoid the cancers of falsehood and corruption? How do you even know what you were born into?

Were you born into a bad country, a bad family, a bad economy, a bad location, a bad time? Or good ones?

Isn't it funny (not) that we tend to judge others as if they thought like we did and understood walking in our shoes? If I care about you, I assume you care about me. If you "friend" me on Facebook are you really a friend?

How do I know what you were born into?

How do we trust? It is getting less and less easy to trust. Why?

Funny… our soldiers in Afghanistan trust each other. Why?

Once upon a time we were all born into the same values. A handshake was trusted. Your word was trusted. What has happened? What have we abandoned to get us here?

We now have to trust the indecipherable fine print. We have to trust that government will protect us.

What are our children being born into? Where am I?

"Hate Evil"

I don't know about you… but I hate evil.

We hate so many things these days. There are people we hate. There are crimes we hate. I am not saying we don't love, too. But this writ is about hate… I hate attitudes that say the glass is half empty, where everything has a negative cast to it. It has taken me a lifetime to truly find the power of the positive and hope.

We hate people telling us what to do. We hate selfish people. We hate corruption. I hate bureaucracy. I hate fine print.

Well, you get the message. Bet you could give me a long list.

There are so many things to protect. It is our job to define what is really important. It is our individual job to define what we stand for. I fear we are putting off this discussion with ourselves as it would involve commitment. What do you stand for? What lines are there that cannot be crossed?

"We hate so many things these days."

One major line is evil. Do you accept evil or is it just an unpleasant circumstance that needs a law to make it illegal next time??? Without clear definition of good and evil we become meaningless. Without meaning.

I can attest that good is really good. When someone does something unselfish, when someone helps someone else, when we serve others… I find that really good. That has to be protected.

When evil intrudes I get mad. I hate evil. I hate the evil that keeps people from helping one another. I hate evil that starves people. I hate evil that keeps the poor poor. Sometimes I feel that it is government that keeps the poor poor. Certainly many governments do.

Why can't we get a black and white grip on evil? Why can't we just say "no" more often? Why do we have to parse and debate responsibility? Start at home by saying "no" to your children. Teach them the value of "no."

Then teach them to hate evil. Evil hurts people. Evil steals opportunity from us.

Then teach them what is good. Teach them to fight for good.

I will even die for good. I hate evil. It is not going away.

Ok, I have an issue with evil.

Today I am going to tweet really bad things about evil.

"Hillary for President"

Hillary for President.

OK... I had to use this title to get you to read this... Yep, I tricked you... but did I?

What are the requirements to be a good leader? Does it hold for both business and politics? How about educators, scientists, humanitarians??? Do we have different standards for different leaders, executives, officers???

Well, I'll bet that today they have to be insensitive... have no feelings... that's what I think. For if they show feelings the media will be all over them. Criticism is in vogue and is the fast info food of the masses. Masses??? That's you and me. Scour backgrounds for anything. Vilify and roast at 6:30 PM. If one has a human tic or uniqueness see if you can make fun of it or SNL it... Where is class? Where is respect? Who is responsible for what? Is there anything we won't text???

"Mocked almost sounds Biblical."

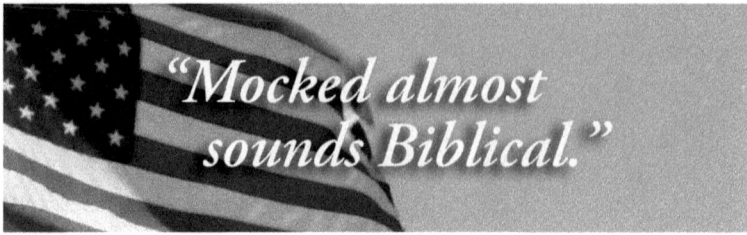

How much fun is it to be a President and be continuously mocked by the opposition? Mocked? Mocked almost sounds Biblical.

If you listened to the mocking you would think that every President has been a buffoon. Has anyone sat in their skins? Has anyone listened to all the expert advice they have been offered by those surrounding them, the media, and anyone who can reach them? Hindsight for us makes it easy to mock mercilessly with chosen perspective and bias meant to drive home the still elusive truth. Were we in the oval office when one man had to make a decision to which there was no assurance? Hawk or dove... we won't know for a 100 years. Invade? Drop the atomic bomb? Increase sanctions? What do we really know in our lifetimes???

Ok... we have established you had better not have feelings.

Now, most important is that you must have experience and lots of it. I would hope you have governed, run a business, held office, and had developed communication skills. Without all these you are in trouble. Good luck. History will not be kind to the novice. Let's make the Presidency PG-60.

As they say in real estate... location, location, location. As we should say in the oval office... integrity, integrity, integrity. Character defines every moment. A past can have its spots but can also be a powerful sculptor of character. Hide nothing and win everything.

In fact, who can throw the first stone? And why do we act like we can???

Hillary is running.

Who can run against her with class?

"Rear View Mirror"

Cruising along in life wondering what is next? Around the next turn? In the next meeting? On the next face? In the next text?

When you are young all looks so bright and promising. Health and vigor dominates and assures that all can be managed. Protected from harm the rainbows all have pots of gold.

Then as young adults, wars and conflict enter lives. Some people do turn out to be bad. The beckoning of pleasure and avoidance both seductively lead one down different paths. Self centered… one charges forward… People get hurt. Feelings are trespassed. We become responsible for things we wish we weren't.

Full speed ahead. Through the front looking glass life still looks amazing. So many people have so many great things. There is no reason we can't have them too. Work hard, make money, and be happy.

> *"Through the front looking glass life still looks amazing."*

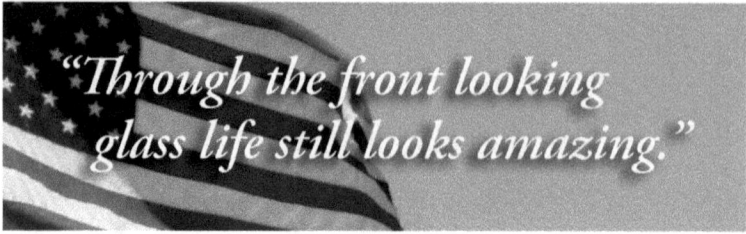

But as the years go by things build up in the rear view mirror. There are mistakes we made that privately still bother us. In fact they just don't go away. They don't wash off easily. They hide deep down. Pleasure only obscures them for a day or so. Why won't they go away? Why does having possibly hurt someone gnaw at us? Why...? Aren't we in control of everything...? We can decide what to think about... right? If one chooses to harden oneself and pretend they never happened then we become insincere, false, insecure, and a non-person... certainly someone not worthy of trust. Yes the rear view mirror starts to take over and we can no longer drive straight and give all our focus to the needs of the present and future...

We need a wiper for the rear view mirror. It is called forgiveness. It's available in special stores for free. But they are not in Google. They have to be found on foot. Not-quitting. Enduring the uncertainty of an unfamiliar journey. Our only compass is found within.

This requires of each of us to reconsider all choices made. To revisit our core and re-determine what we stand for and what we will not stand.

Most dismiss such a thought as folly. For them there is no journey and the assurance of insignificant growth and reward.

The rearview mirror is frosted with regret. The wiper is the heat of Truth that is kindled in forgiveness. Then a quick glance will affirm that the past is clear and the way ahead is without distraction.

We need to be fueled with the truth and wisdom from the past, not the pain.

Full speed ahead. Humility in tow.

I now know where I am going and how to get there.

"Hi Mom"

"Hi Mom."

How come whenever I look at the Today Show and they pan the people outside all you see are "Hi Mom" signs?

My first reaction is what about us dads??? Then I reflected that a mother's eye never leaves the child. Point taken. Discussion moot.

But what about the "Hi Mom" signs that don't appear in the rest of the world? Think about it. I am going to make this disturbing.

We hear all the clatter in America about justified women's rights. We have come a long way… OK, but we are traitors to the cause internationally. Media and activists show no spine or conviction or honor when they do not take up the cause in Africa, the Far East, or the Middle East. Women's rights??? There are none. Brutality, hard and soft, is perpetrated by the male dominated cultures. The insane, male/egocentric obsession with control over the female is a cancer on the dignity of man.

"Where are our talented feminist activists?"

I am sure that under the guise of Human Rights there is a category for women. Under the guise of state-sponsored political correctness there is a whitewash of this gender injustice... no... excuse me... gender holocaust!

This topic is not on the table... Or if it gets there... time is not left on the agenda...

Why do we chastise ourselves for any transgression when what is being done to women in other countries is revolting? Where are our talented feminist activists? Oh, sure there is the occasional afternoon interview show that shares the plight of an African tragedy that a woman survived to tell the story...

Why can't there be a war declared against female abuse? Why?

Of course, we have a hard enough time determining who is a terrorist... Or protecting the sensitivities of the proven criminal. Why can't we use drones against regimes that brutalize women? Let's fight for real causes, not geopolitical dead-end streets.

Why can't all women on our planet walk their streets with security and freedom? Let a veil be a garment of choice, not of fear.

This is where I want to use my large capacity magazines.

Why aren't there "Hi Mom" signs in Tehran?

"18 and Older"

What should the age be for what? I repeat! What should the age be for what? Who decides??? Who decides??? Should we decide who decides? When can we change who decides? When can we change what? Do we have any say in anything? When will we decide to agree on something?

When I was young you had to be 21 to drink, but not to lose your life in combat. When I was young you could start driving at 16. That's about it.

Who has the list of ages at which you can do what? When is a child still a child? If a child can perpetrate a heinous act when is he responsible for it?

A lot of tough questions to be thrown at the judicial system. We appear to be abrogating decisions to codes and regulations which are becoming more and more complex. Lawyers are becoming regulations clericals, parsing fine print and passing on elaborate recommendations to their superiors who are experts at same. We lowly citizens then

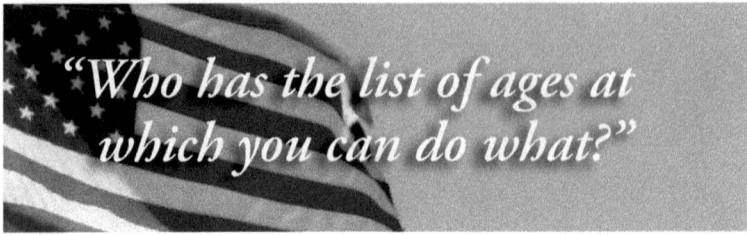

must be able to unravel their articulations and extract direction. Except we can't without an attorney.

It is now more noble to protect the criminal than the victim.

I think I read recently that the cutoff age for some issue was 12. If you are 11 then you are safe… My how times have changed. How does a parent be a parent anymore without knowing all the rules and regulations?

Since we have discredited religion, the responsibility for protecting ourselves falls on government. Makes sense, except we are heading down the path where there will be more government employees than private business employees. But is it not business that pays the taxes that funds the government?

I don't get it?

Glad I am over 18.

"Go Away"

"Go away."

How many people and situations do you wish would just go away? Maybe someone is telling you something to do? How about your father? How about your boss? How about your drill sergeant? How about the IRS?

I'll bet your life is full of instances which you wish would disappear. How about some body fat, or acne, or disease, or handicap? Why doesn't anything happen when you say "Go away?" Think about it. Why can't your bills go away?

Things can go away if you stop telling them to. You see, the problem is often you.

You/we create our own problems. It is our behavior and approach that needs change. Quite possibly, things and people will treat us differently. Maybe if we treat our problems with more respect they might reciprocate. Easy to say... But this often means we must change in how we respond to and perceive things. The more positive we are,

> *"The more positive we are,
> the clearer a path becomes."*

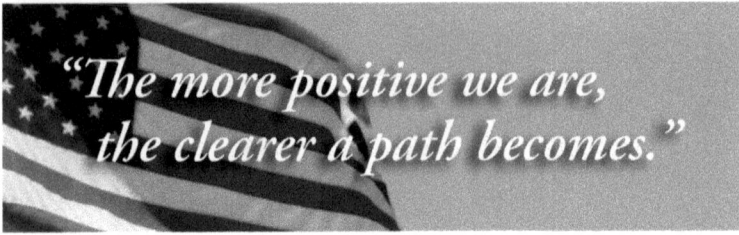

the clearer a path becomes. But the only real solution to respect is to live in Truth. Abandon self-centered activity and replace with a "service" approach. Like "How may I help you, life?" LOL.

People are drawn to the honest and humble. That is our goal. To find out how to be that. They won't say "Go away" to us any longer. And likewise we will do the same.

Respect evil. For what it is.

Define it. Define good. Define yourself. Then be true to good and see where it takes you. Fight for good. Die for good. Mean something. Draw your own red lines.

When there is trouble don't go away. Face it head-on with conviction. Be an example of saying that things matter… and that things must be dealt with, not dismissed.

On a long run pain will not go away, but it can be mitigated and put to the side by the vision of a finish line's reward within grasp.

All in life is within grasp with hope and faith.

"Go away," fear and ignorance. I am better than you. I can change.

With divine help.

"On My Sleeve"

Have you ever heard that? "Don't wear your religion on your sleeve??"

I have. I remember being corrected when I was young. Forgot where. But it stuck. You know... don't force your beliefs on someone else. Good advice. Hey, people are always giving all kinds of advice... isn't this forcing what they believe on one another??? Gets confusing.

What government agency defines what one can say and what one cannot? Or can anyone say anything to anyone? This is Constitution territory.

What exactly can you wear on your sleeve? Does that mean what you stand for? Are you supposed to suppress your convictions?

Well, as I look around, everyone is wearing so much stuff on their sleeves that appears to indicate what is important to them. Let's start with gossip and scandal. Never stops coming out of mouths, whispered and yelled. How about

"Don't wear your religion on your sleeve."

objections??? How about every sort of cause, good and bad??

It's not about the sleeve, dummy... it is about the mouth. You are defined by what you say. Thank God we have Facebook and Twitter and texting. At least now there are records of all we have said... all we have put on our sleeves.

So back to that awful word "religion." This was the start of all this gibberish.

We are who we are. And we wear ourselves on our sleeves. We don't wear religion... that is nonsense. But what we care about we wear on our sleeves.

Words really don't "cut it" anymore. They have just become rap... spilling out in endless repetitive type and song. The real sleeve is what one does... one's acts.

You are noticed if you help someone else. And if you hurt someone... you are noticed. It is your acts that define you. It is your excess and mistakes that define you until you undo them with humility and forgiveness. The goal is to have a white sleeve. A sleeve that only serves and helps others.

Where do you find it? Where can you buy it? Not on Amazon.

Maybe in some really old writings written by a bunch of misfits who redeemed themselves with sacrifice and good acts. They are dead now. Their Word is not.

"Have Our Churches Failed Us?"

I know someone who goes there who sleeps with"…
or… "That church is people who think they are better
than us"… or… "That denomination is so full of rules.
Forget it"… or… "Everyone looks at what you are
wearing"… or… "They ask you to do things I would not be
comfortable with."

Have you heard or thought this before??? Bet you have…
All valid excuses to stay away from church. What is going
on? Have our churches failed us???

Have you ever heard of kids who were raised strict? Where
their parents set boundaries and promoted values?? Where
parents not only said no but also disciplined??? Nine
times out of ten these kids ended up successful. That is my
experience. I say wow! To strong work ethics, integrity,
honesty, humility, and no sense of entitlement. Then there
are those who had no parents, but were influenced by some

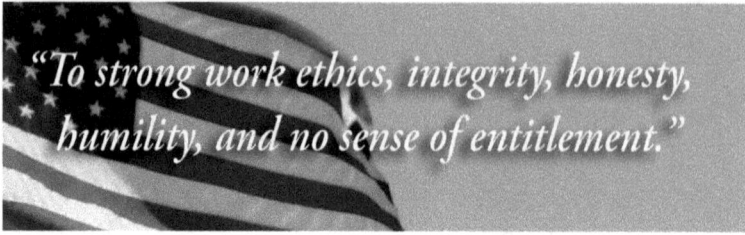

"To strong work ethics, integrity, honesty, humility, and no sense of entitlement."

seed of good, compassion, and morality along the way. They had the same appreciation for the value of work and of giving of oneself. As for the kids who indulged in the symphonies of permissiveness...??? Well, you know the story... And they... don't.

Our world used to know what the difference was between black and white. Today, all hail the grey where all accountability and responsibility goes to the "excuse". Our media wallows in analysis of a system that failed the individual. Certainly not the individual failing the system. Are we not tired of listening to the blame games, parties blaming the other, leaders blaming the blamed? What folly!!! And this is our youth and what we all allow under the guise of entertainment and news. There must be a reason why Johnny hit Mary. Call the psychiatrist.

Everything is grey now. No need to worry. Long live the Grey. Media rejoice, so much to talk about...Talk, talk, talk.

We have become obsessed with the feelings of others. Think about it... Way beyond common sense caring.

Protecting feelings has become a religion for those who want no religion. We worry about what someone else thinks of us and adjust our behavior to address that fantasy. Ninety-nine percent of the time we are just wrong. It is idiotic to think that we know what someone else is thinking. Most minds are so introverted and do not care about what you think at any given moment unless texting, of course... LOL. Heaven forbid if we call something evil.

Evil does not exist. It exists only as "socio-economic aberrations" to be cured by sensitive diplomacy and deniability. If you admit that evil exists then you might have to address the concept of the Devil...Oops that is going into science fiction...

Speaking of fiction... how come the New York Times Book Review cannot comprehend or really categorize the #1 continuous Best Seller of all time? Is it fiction...??? They believe it to be but won't say so... hmmm... If they call it non-fiction...??? Hmmm? Then they would be endorsing it??? And they would be mocked by their own... So I guess the Bible has little to do with anything other than the far right conservative zealot's need for religion???

The need for White has never been greater. White stands for values, beliefs, borders, love, and commitment thereto. The most admired people have real, not material, core values. These are the ones to trust. Ok... where do you find out about such things? In Churches. Hello??? Who is failing who? Is it we who are failing our churches??? Next time you see a Church person go hug them. You need it more than they do. And if they are Christian, all the better to me. What is wrong with an opinion? Let's celebrate them and move on.

"Leading Cause"

There are so many leading causes of death that you can't keep track.

Most recent is texting while driving.

Yes, for teenagers. Who would have thought?

Take a look at the morning influxes into high schools and watch students walk through the front doors without looking up. LOL. Multi-tasking professionals...walking, talking, and texting. The new "Me-Centric" minority has become the majority in this new fatal classification.

In the seductive stampede for affirmation in a non-affirming secular world individuals of all ages bow their heads to the new reality... the screen of the cell phone. New reality or should I offer... deity??? Hmmm...

In any case, lives are lost when we look down. As long as "friends" respond and send pictures you are validated and your ego satiated. The new spiritual milkshake. Full of ego calories and confidence shots.

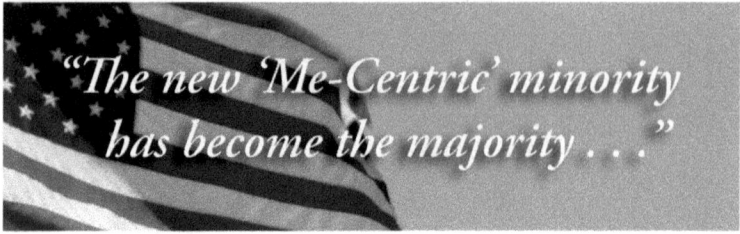

Now back to driving. I have to fight the urge to keep the phone on the seat. My new car does it all by some gal in the dash who answers my questions and places phone calls. But this is a luxury. Look at the car next to you at the stop light. Look at the car monetarily swerving.

We are drunk with ourselves, not alcohol. The new drug is "Me" and we cannot get enough of it…

The new rehab has to be a facility stripped of phones, computers, and mirrors. This will allow one to be immersed in the tranquility of nothingness.

This will provide an opportunity to "look up".

Cure guaranteed.

"Street Me"

Look at a city on any map. Any city. No… better yet go to Google Earth and type in "Me Street." It exists… Well, at least I am not making things up…

There are many streets in life to choose from… or paths, if you will. Every intersection requires a choice or a plan. Turn right, or turn left. Turn right or turn wrong. Or full speed ahead a couple of miles to the next intersection… A lot of roads dead-end, but if there is no sign we make the mistake and end up at the end. Turn around, retrace our steps until we get back to the intersection… curse at the lack of a sign, and go the other way. So many dead-ends. So much wasted time. So many wasted years.

We keep on choosing our turns as long as we are in control of our car. I like cars with sexy exhaust sounds and a lot of horsepower and tight suspensions. It makes getting to the dead-ends fun anyway.

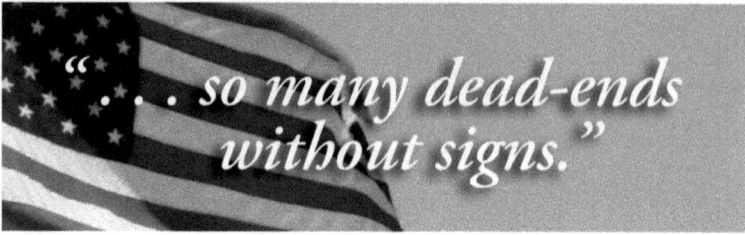

"... so many dead-ends without signs."

Couldn't figure out why there were so many dead-ends without signs. Unless I overlooked them???

Now that I have put 100,000's miles on all kinds of cars over my years, I finally have stopped making wrong turns. I finally think I have found the road without a dead-end sign on it.

To this point it has all been "Street Me." Meaning throw the streets at me and I can handle it, I can drive them. Flat tire. Overheating. Dropped a gear. I got places, but they didn't turn out to be what I wanted. I hurt some people along the way with my reckless driving on "Street Me."

Where was AAA when I needed them? I wanted more direction. Life needs an itinerary. Life needs directions. Life needs a GPS. And a radar detector. I could have been saved a lot of tickets and guilt.

Yes, life needs an itinerary. Where you say where you start and keystroke in where you are going. Picking the safest and surest route, not necessarily the fastest.

AAA just gave me roads. Streets are not enough. We have to have speed limits and only the best highway. I want more time to do good. I want more time to make a difference to others. I want more time to ensure I never hurt anyone again. I want US 1… spelled US You. I want to be driving on "Street You"… That is the street where I serve others, where I serve you. I want to make sure there is a dead-end sign on "Street Me".

I need the right itinerary. They hand them out in Church.

"Judge and Jury"

This is going to be so much fun.

I know none of you have ever been judgmental. You have never looked down on anyone regardless of how they looked or acted. I am sure your face always reflected impartiality and understanding.

There are other cultures and persuasions. There are other interpretations of right and wrong. I know you feel uncomfortable as soon as you feel an opinion forming. You are an enlightened citizen who never judges what the media or others might. Whenever you read a text criticizing someone you withhold judgment… while admonishing the sender for pre-judging. You are just good. In fact, you are perfect. There is no wrong until a fair and carefully selected jury decides. In time, in due course.

The problem is that we have constructed a courtroom in our own head. We never tell anyone, but we are the Chief Justice of Our Own Supreme Court that comes to order

"We have to be known for being humble."

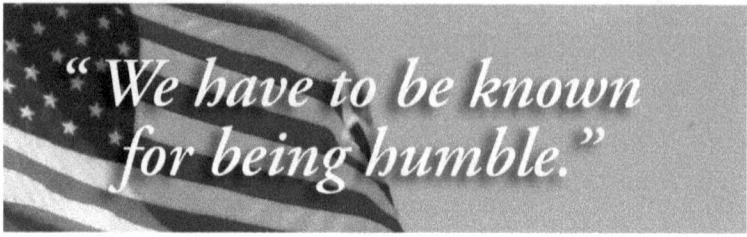

whenever requested. This can be characterized as "headstrong" or "headwrong???"

Gossip and scandal help condition us to instant decision, instant jury ruling. There are no recesses allowed. We move quickly from one tidbit to another, accruing decisions and sentences before our mind's ink is dry. Yes we all know it is our nature to judge all day long. Jury selection not needed. Just let me see someone and I have an instant opinion and it is soon cemented by texting. Judge and jury… that is who we are until we close the court and open our collective heart.

Did we know all the circumstances about that person? Never. Do we want to be judged without a jury? Never. Do we want to be able to correct a judgment against us? You bet.

To be judged fairly we have to start by judging fairly. We have to be known as a very principle-driven honest people. We have to be known for only caring about Truth. We have to be known for only caring about others. We have to be known for being humble.

Tall order.

"Court is now in session." "Would the accused please rise? Yes, all of you. Yes, all of humanity. Yes, you Presidents, Kings, and CEO's too."

"You are all found guilty of judging one another."

"Sentencing will be next Wednesday after you have all read the Bible."

"One Word"

We have become so fond of words. We are going nuts with all kinds of words and creating new ones by the dozens every day. The dictionaries are being forced to expand because so many spins and twists are put into sounds. Try and decipher pop music for starters. But they're all words that communicate contemporary complexities to the newborn.

Pundits and hosts and commentators fully over-explain every bit of news and trivia. We are lost in the sea of new words and old words with new meaning. Constants are being challenged. Rules are being redefined. Furthermore, our government is fully complicit in its own expansions of fine print and finite interpretation of the infinite.

Voice prompts have dehumanized discourse. Talk to a robot or talk to a customer service center in the Far East and you will pull hair out trying to find the new clarity.

"sensitivity."

Interact with a business and you will no longer find a one-page contract or agreement. Turn to a second page and another and another and sign at the bottom. Their lawyers have covered every imaginable liability to insure you are screwed and they are not. Fine print? Red tape? The words have got you. They declare the winner.

It is amazing how smiley everything is until it gets to words on paper. Would you like some water??? You had better grab it as you are going to get dry mouth trying to read anything out loud these days.

One word? What in the heck does that mean?

"Trust me." When I hear that I no longer do. It is now a sign of deceit!!!

We can no longer just say "yes" or "no." There has to be a qualification. What do you mean by a "yes?" What are you really saying when you say "no" now???

One-word dialogue has to be reinvented. It has to become counter-culture or trendy to be accepted again. Of course so does "good." That is one great word that has been so parsed that it means little. Now there is one word that is much more powerful these days… It is "sensitivity." Being sensitive puts you on the vanguard of heroism.

Sensitivity means a lot in Damascus as in Tehran or anywhere where feelings and concern are alive… Washington???

How about "No" meaning "NO" again.

It hasn't changed in the Marine Corps. Let's have it mean something in the home again.

Let's say "Yes" to standing for something.

Let's say "Yes" to "I want my country back."

Let's say "Yes" to making things simple again.

Let's say "Yes Mom, Yes Dad."

"57 Virgins"

Why do men want so much?

Back in the beginnings of civilization or even existence, the male of our species was the provider and protector. He was in charge of life and death, rules and punishment. The woman was in charge of birth, nurturing and pleasure. Over the millenniums more and more rules were established to protect order and fragile justice. Life was tribal, then cultures formed creating new interpretations of old rules.

Not all that much fine print on scrolls? Men fought the wars. Killed off enough to rule for a while until the cycle repeated itself. Woman was always second and mainly voiceless. Pleasure for the male was insured by laws…harsh laws… which still stand in significant parts of the world today. Look at the headlines.

Women's rights are still at a standstill in Africa, the Middle East, and the Orient… It ain't right. Meanwhile we dither about our glass ceilings…

> ## "Rules should be made for human beings, not genders."

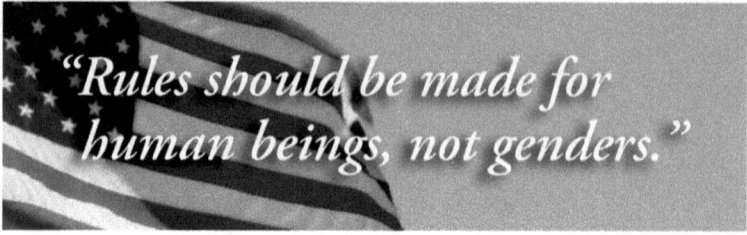

I don't need to be promised 57 virgins to go to heaven. That is sexist too. I don't dream about flopping around naked on clouds in exotic heavenly pleasures. Anyone who promises such is lying. I just want the assurance I get to see my mom and dad again... and get to know their parents, and their parents' parents. I believe I can not kill anyone if I want to get there. I believe I have to ask for forgiveness to qualify. I want to be able to receive forgiveness from all who I had hurt. It may take a little time... but that would be heaven to me.

Rules should be made for human beings, not genders.

They should all be updated and simplified so they can easily be texted and shared on Facebook. Get governments out of the rule business. It seems like they are adding amendments and qualifications weekly. Who can keep track of all the fine print. Sign here??... and be held accountable in cyber-space for eternity.

Oops... I didn't read the fine print.

It is only two old virgins.

"Sin is a Stupid Word"

Sin is such a stupid word.

Why does anyone ever use it? It is like church people to just throw it around trying to make everyone feel guilty. Yes, this problem can be solved easily by just deleting the word from everything. Maybe make it illegal to even say it, since it's so accusatory. Maybe local governments could issue tickets and fines for violators.

It is a sin to make others feel guilty. In fact, most of the wrongs considered sins should be re-examined in light of the new laws. Maybe a lot of people in jail were wrongly accused because of the word "sin". The courts will sure be busy sorting this one out. But it is about time! Long overdue. Think of all the feelings that have been hurt. For no stupid reason…

Let's be positive and now only focus on good things. In fact, let's list all that is good and make laws to protect them. That sounds like a good and proper road to go on. Legislatures arise! Enact the obvious. Make it illegal to not do good.

"Make it illegal to not do good."

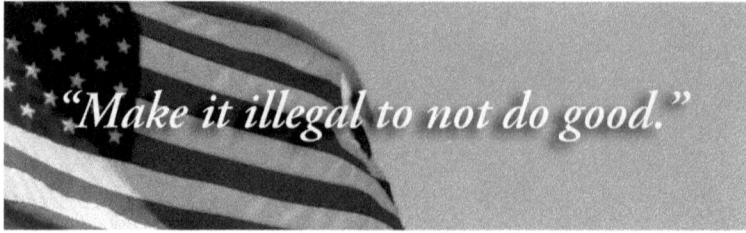

Ok, when someone does something that is not good what do we call it? How about keeping it simple? Just call it "bad." But there are so many ways to be bad that we have to control that. Let's revisit our good laws and make sure all possible bad acts are covered. We will deal with bad thoughts later. Who creates bad? Let's catch the creators and perpetrators. Of course, we need police to provide protection and arrest capability. Let's profile bad-doers. Let's head them off before they commit bad. They really should have no rights.

Let's further define bad. What is it? Anything which hurts someone else is bad. Or hurts their feelings... Anything which fosters inequality is bad. Anything which judges is bad. Anything which limits my social networking is bad. Anything which tells me what to do is bad. Whew, this is getting too complicated. Why is "I" the middle letter of sin...???

There has to be some kind of "good" compass to guide one through this maze. Let's look for a Book that is just about good.

Maybe "bad" is a stupid word too.

"The Voice"

Doggone it! The Voice has become my favorite escape show. Monday and Tuesday nights at 8 PM don't bother calling.

This is about the music of life. New voices singing their hearts out for fame and escape from obscurity. The judges are wonderful and their smiles and positive guidance sparkles with genuineness... Blake Shelton, Usher, Adam Levine, and the lovely Shakira float my boat. Nice to know that you are being judged and coached by fun and good guys. How often do you ever feel you are being judged fairly, much less by caring people? How often? Criticism couched in caring. That's why this show stands above so many. I don't care if Blake drinks... I do too.

We hear so many stories of coming from poverty and abandonment to get to the auditions and show. Then ultimately being put on the stage of judgment in front of the whole world! All but one will not advance. But you get

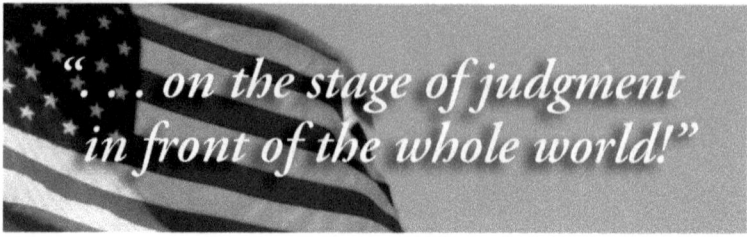

the feeling that all are being judged fairly. Anyway it is just a TV show.

When I die I want to be judged by someone as good as these. It want it to be ultra-fair. Who is really capable of this??? Who???

We can liken our lives to songs. There is our own unique melody. There are our own unique lyrics, our life of words for which to be held accountable. The melody is all the acts that made our music. Sometimes off pitch or too this or that. Sometimes our life song stopped as we gave up or detoured into self-centric waste and excess.

Did we ever try to find a coach? And who was it? Did we ever acknowledge that we might need help in life? A mentor? Not a therapist, but a real guide?? We are so self-assured that we are reluctant to ask for help. Our ego demands that we solve everything ourselves. Ego blinders... they keep us like the race horse from seeing what is actually all around us.

Every person is so self absorbed that they wall off their coach, their inner Voice. Have you ever, just once, stopped and talked to yourself about what is the best or right thing to do? I have. And something deep inside speaks. Do you listen?

It speaks the truth. Most often we ignore it because it isn't the easiest solution...except that... later... in hindsight... it is.

We all have a conscience that exists to protect and guide us. We can call it all kinds of names to make it go away... But it is always there, no matter how deep we try to hide it.

Well, all the votes start coming in. A lot of people don't vote for us for sure. But if we listened to our inner voice many did.

OK Pearly Gates I am ready.

Bring Him on...

"Memorial Day"

Our flag flies at half mast. Our flag.

The flag of the United States of America.

Our flag allows us to debate, criticize and protest as much as we want without fear of persecution. It is amazing how much we love to criticize. Media and social networks are ablaze with condemnation. Oh yes, there are stories of good works… but those headlines are stolen by scandal and criticism, however intellectually cloaked.

Freedom of speech is the greatest threat to freedom throughout the world. What we take for granted is feared elsewhere. We are under attack by radical this and that because freedom of speech will destroy their power. Terrorism is applied to those willing to speak. Sad.

Graves freshly dug and graves of 1776 abound with sacrifice and tragedy. Tragedy if the life was lost for no reason. Those of us who live have to make those losses have meaning by how we conduct ourselves. The veteran is not

> " ... *amazing how much we love to criticize.*"

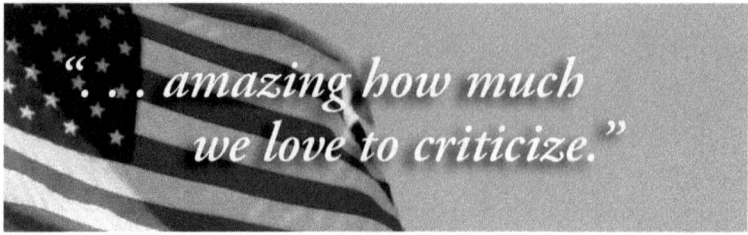

that outspoken for he knows the horror of war and the value of freedom. We all too often mock and abuse it.

It is time we bring dignity and respect back into our lexicon. Yes ma'am, yes sir. Yes Mother, yes Father.

Our hypocrisy is so much more visible these days. Look at the killings and the excesses of our behavior. Look at pictures of crowds these days and how fat we have become. We mock those who differ. We mock religion... Respect for elders??? Forget it. They are just old people who are not relevant.

On Memorial Day we are bowing our heads to our cell phones and not to those who made this land of cell phones free.

The tear on the eye of the Veteran reflects the light of Truth.

It knows evil and it knows folly.

Thank you for your service.

"Wanted"

The FBI Most Wanted poster. Ever imagined your face on it? How about posters that say "Wanted Dead Or Alive?"

There is not one human being that does not want to be wanted. Why do women dress with fashion and allure? Always checking in the mirror to see if their "look" is "wantable..." And I have seen guys at the Y checking their hair after they shave, turning their head side to side. Why?... you know... it is the "Want-Syndrome." Flirting because you want someone to like you. We desperately want to be wanted. The extreme is the celebrity who basks in adoration that satiates their intrinsic insecurity. But wait a second... we are all insecure from the git-go. Why are we so attached to our mothers? Because they loved us unconditionally regardless of our selfishness. They made us feel wanted. God love 'em. In fact they were the first person that let us feel that we were worth being wanted. And we chase that need until we die.

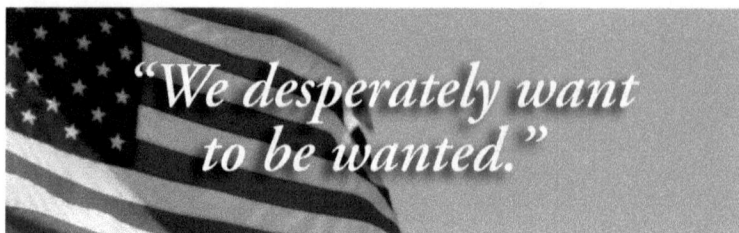

Today our texting and our Facebook-type pursuits are all about being wanted. Generally we have to make someone else feel wanted and then they reflexively reciprocate. Cell phones should be renamed "wantphones."

If one has a loving family upbringing, one is blessed to be less dependent on want for character development and autonomy. If the upbringing reflects respect for values and discipline then freedom from want is easier to find.

But life has many unsuspected circumstances that bring hurt. We withdraw into the pain as we desperately seek solace and a compelling need to be wanted. Addictions and tragic behavior temporarily fill some voids. Dishonesty and self-centered acts provide cover. Some turn to crime. Some turn to lies and indifference to truth. These are the souls who need to be wanted the most. Ironic, is it not?

A face on a poster or in a lineup reveals one who needed to be wanted so much that they made sure they never could be.

I don't want to be wanted.

I just want to help people who want a helping hand.

I just want to do enough good that God wants me.

"Unity"

Something amazing has happened in Naples, Florida.

A phenomenon that exists not elsewhere.

The letters to the lucky editor are 95% in favor of repealing the name ARTIS, which was so artfully conceived to replace "The Phil" or our Philharmonic Center For The Arts.

Democrats and Republicans are united.

When we all get together we can accomplish the impossible.

My gripe is not with this cause, but with women's rights.

Why are no voices raised?

Why are all the male dominated cultures given a pass when it comes to the abuse of women and children?

Where is the liberal media?

Where is the conservative media?

Why are girls sold into marriage?

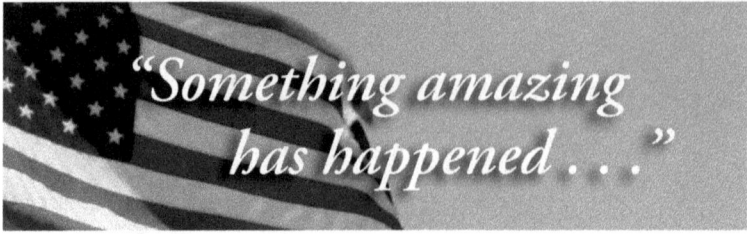

> "Something amazing
> has happened . . . ."

Why are laws in existence which forbid women to do this and that?

Why is rape ignored?

Why is the woman victim the guilty one?

Why are our consciences so selective? What bubble do we live in?

Where are the activists?

Shame on them and shame on us all as we revel in Washington scandals but not human ones.

We deserve ARTIS... Any Reason To Ignore Sensibility.

Can't we move on?

For the sake of the arts?

What's abuse anyway?

"Right Man"

How in the world does a woman find the right man? Mr. Right. The guy who will provide and protect, be faithful and caring. Always ensuring no harm will come to her and their family. To nurture and love, providing the home from which to grow and contribute to mankind... Character, integrity, and values are essential... Looks never hurt either.

Does a woman have a right to find the right man? In the United States she sure does. Does she have a right to choose? To pursue happiness?

What about the man? How does he find the right woman, the one who will cornerstone her family and raise the children? In a marriage is the woman an equal? Big question. What about obey?

What happens if you don't marry the right person? What happens if Mr. Right is Mr. Wrong?

Marriage is becoming confusing. Diffused. Regulated. There are cultures where it is upside down and children are assigned to grievous unions.

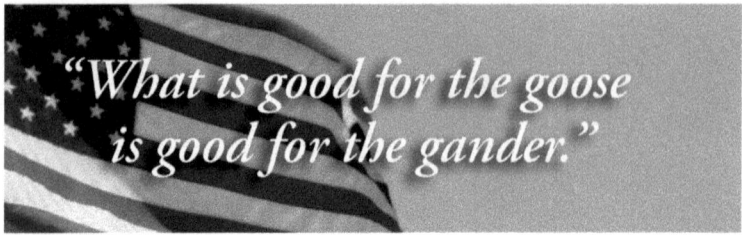

Why shouldn't sexy men be told to cover up their faces too?

We have an expression… "What is good for the goose is good for the gander." Hmmm…

Should there be equalities or not?

Should not gender abuse be better defined? Should not the United States be more specific about women's rights? Should not our country be the greatest place in the world for women to live? Are we not already proud of the advancements made?

Why do we hold climate change higher than women's rights?

Which is killing more children?

Will Mr. Right stop getting things wrong?

"PDTMWTD"

Our mother gave birth. And we became us… Dad was a minor player in the miraculous creation. Yes, our "me" was formed at that first breath and scream. And from then on we tested our boundaries… Got spanked a little… corrected behavior and charged on into life and identity formation… With little clue as to where we were going or how to get there.

Fast forward to our teens where the vigor of our body outpaced the maturity of our emotions. We felt life and we believed wholeheartedly in ourselves. We experimented with right and we experimented with wrong. We tried to figure out what was good and what was bad… though bad didn't seem to matter that much as long as it didn't immediately hurt us.

But it was in our teens that PDTMWTD became the first and foremost developed reflex. In fact it is cherished and flexed throughout our life. It is our sacred vow to the

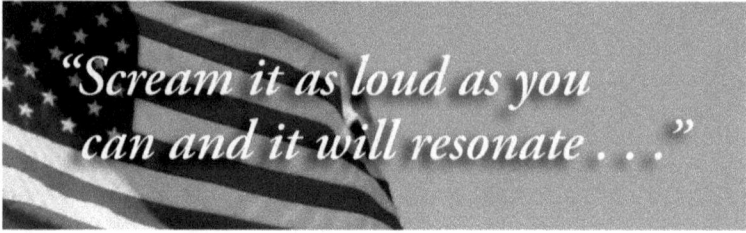

world... "Please Don't Tell Me What To Do." Scream it as loud as you can and it will resonate with the core of your being.

I ask why this expression is so much a part of every person. Advice is so intrusive. Agree? No matter how much you love your child, you had better chill as they DO NOT want to be told what to do. Regardless of their age... LOL.

There has to be a better way to communicate. How about threats? How about gifts? No, neither really work at home, or in politics, or with other countries.

How in the world do you guide someone when you know what they don't?

Firstly, they have to want to listen, they have to ask the questions they don't know how to ask. So forget it. It gets deep here. For the answer lies in trust. When your reflex is PDTMWTD it means you don't trust. You do not trust the advice or the person offering the advice. It is that simple. Nagging is equated with advice. Go away.

I will trust you if your values resonate with mine. Then you may say all you want. Real trust is formed through strong shared values. When we are on the same page about good and evil, humility and arrogance, compassion and service, sin and justice, loving and giving… then real trust forms.

Trust is found in combat. Trust is found in love. Trust is found in sacrifice.

Trust is not easy to come by. One learns this over a lifetime when trusts are broken.

Trust is birthed in the heart. Listening to our heart, really listening to it all the time is the pivotal moment. Hopefully before we have hardened it into meaninglessness. Heart-felt is at the core of being. Being somebody.

PDTMWTD until I am ready. Ready to give my life to trust. To Truth.

You have to tell yourself what to do. And you had better be right.

Godspeed.

"Passion"

Passion defines you. Did you ever think about that?

Do you remember the first time you could not get him or her out of your mind? You were so attracted... Your pulse kicked up a beat... You anxiously waited for the next moment you would see your passion. To most others it was most obvious... even without the blush. But you sure felt the blush inside. In passion all is black and white... compelling you to action with overwhelming emotion in anticipation of that first embrace. People began to know you by this passion. It became your new label.

Well then there is puppy passion. There is nothing like holding a new puppy in your arms. You melt as you assume the role of protector and sublimely slip into love...

But this is nothing like a mother's first look into the eyes of her newborn baby. Eyes that will be linked for eternity. I'd call it passion.

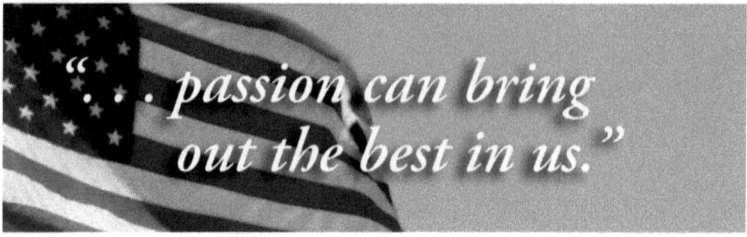

A pilot with his sport plane. Or us with our motorcycle, car, or football team. Passion can be found everywhere. How about at the peak of Mount Everest? Had to take passion to get there.

It follows that passion can bring out the best in us. It stands for an intense personal focus that drives effort to refined excellence and completeness.

Passion is most often distorted by an association with sin. Look at all the infinite number of films and shows dedicated to the passions of flesh... ok sex...

Passions are associated with the pleasing of self. I think this is a critical juncture for every human in life. If there is a transition from self to "unself" more amazing things can happen. It is called growth. Ponder this irony. Think about it.

Our sensual senses complicate who we can be.

Who are the most revered people in history? I contend they are those who made sacrifices for others. Who put themselves aside to help and serve someone else. Think about those people in your life that you admire. Unselfishness and giving are usually the defining traits??? Make a list of all those people who have truly touched you in a positive way... Or, if you must, all those who touched you in a negative way... bet they were selfish...

Who do you want to be like?

The hero gives his life up to save someone.

Self-sacrifice in the face of rough odds. Taking the hit to protect another. Not being afraid to take criticism for something you believe in.

Real passion is found in helping others, not in lusting for them. More shows and time should be devoted to unmasking the unselfish, to praising their courage, to modeling their values.

It takes real Passion to define you... like on the Cross.

Or on your knees with your children...

"Silence"

Silence. Shhhh… "You are on silence." Remember when your teacher or parent used to tell you that? Or… "You be quiet or else…!"

Quiet. Silence. Peace.

In the stillness of quiet one begins to listen… One begins to hear…

We are talking so much these days… Ok… texting… Facebooking… Skyping, etc… in silence… but it really is a roar. Fake silence… But it is funny if you stand back and see how busy we are being silent…

Does this new silent world order portend growth and solution or problems??? Something to think about.

On another note, and more damning, is the silence of cowardice. We can busy ourselves with keyboard activities and not see what is going on around us. We can be brilliant on the small screens that we carry, play and communicate

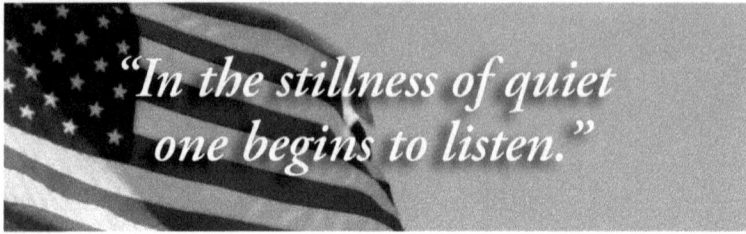

with, but... but... Will it be the new battleground of truth or... Will it be the new battleground avoidance???

At some point our voices have to be heard by ears and action. By vote and reform. The silent majority must be heard out LOUD!!!

Maybe there can be a new government agent called SMD, the Silence Management Directorate? It will advise us when we can and cannot be silent.

I know we all know when we turn our head the other way. When we remain silent about some thing we prefer to ignore. Or some thing we wished did not happen. Or some thing which was not right. "Don't get involved" is the common rationale.

Avoid confrontation... avoid sharing your opinion. Do we know that we have become an avoidance culture? We have chosen to let others decide what is appropriate... We have gotten our PHDs in sensitivity to sensitivity. A Doctorate in inaction.

Silence is becoming our cultural solution to discomfort. In the process silence is sanctioning chaos.

When all choose not to speak out for values and what they truly believe in, evil and injustice will determine the laws and their interpretation.

The question is what kind of silence do I choose to stand for? What are the consequences of individual silence?

There are consequences to speaking out. Courage and conviction are required.

Name three causes. Pick any. List them. Then see which you are not afraid to speak out about. Your silence will say a lot about who you really are and who you have chosen to be.

Your silence sanctions.

It becomes tacit approval by you of what kind of abuses…?

You decide.

"Entertainment"

Entertainment is such a big part of our lives. Since the beginning of "recorded" man entertainment was created as a distraction and panacea for the tribulations of existence.

It became formulated and formalized into crowd-pleasing venues. Bards and magicians to gladiators in arenas. But more and more it made fun of convention and titillated the senses with sensual innuendo if not brazenness. Playboy Magazine or Housewives of Beverly Hills are new standards of achievement.

Evil is more entertaining than good. I remember when TV and movies were mostly good in the 50's. Humor without sex, stories without murder, news with purpose… all now lost in the rush for ratings. Nice to grow up in. Parents had so relatively little to worry about.

Is there more good than evil in entertainment? It is really your choice. Your choice to say what is entertainment for your family. In fact parents are the only safety valve left

for society. But they are so barraged by advice and regulations and peer pressure that they may become the next endangered species.

There is a great amount of good and wholesome entertainment available. From history to nature there is positive inspiration available. But how does it compete with the latest mass murder? Channels are switched at breaking news...

Tornado just killed...??? Just killed the good entertainment...

Censorship? Who determines what is good or bad? Who? It has to be you. Avoid it and hidden chaos will take over.

Entertainment is seductive. It is so easy to pass it off as benign rather than as a powerful conditioning phenomenon. Use it correctly and make it value-driven and you can shape foundations and encourage greatness. But... if we yield to its sugar and marketing acumen it will be the apple of Eve. It is so hard to undo a bad education. It is so hard to regain innocence.

When is old enough old enough?

When is abuse so subtle that it is not called abuse?

When is abuse so hidden that it can't be seen?

Do we need entertainment police?

Does PG really mean anything anymore?

Who looks out for our souls?

Walt Disney where are you?

Who is championing good over evil?

Can't anyone define evil and tell us it is bad?

Who has that authority now that we have disqualified religion?

Entertainment abuse must be stopped.

"Mistakes"

"I knew I shouldn't have done that!" "When will I ever learn???" "I told you not to do that!!!" "Why did you even say that???" "Because you did that people were hurt."

How do you right a wrong? How do you do right rather than wrong? And who gets to say what is right?

When you are young you don't want to make a mistake because you may get punished by your parents... that is... if you are lucky enough to have them these days. Because if you don't big mistakes were made. And you are paying a price for something that you had no control over...

In school if you make a mistake you get a lower grade. Conversely if you don't... you get A's! Seems like reward goes to the "mistakeless???"

What happens if you make a mistake and you are a pilot? What happens if you make a mistake and you are a Priest?

You see, on our planet, everyone makes mistakes. It's going to happen. From speeding ticket to divorce, the potential for mistake is infinite.

With so many mistakes in our history one would wonder why we are still here…?

So many people drag their mistakes along with them for so long. Their private identity is the guilt from their mistakes. However, study the respected and you will find that the respected turned their mistakes into knowledge. Or… they turned the mistakes perpetrated by others on them into assets. They chose not to quit. They chose to always find a positive road.

Why are so many from broken homes successful when they have every reason to give up? No one from a broken home should get anywhere, right??? No one who has been sinned against should be able to heal or forgive, right?

But they do heal. And they are all around you. If you think you have a bum rap, seek them out and find out otherwise.

There is an unofficial support group for every hurt not yet defined. Look around.

Those hurt can become the healers.

Life is a fight against hurt, against evil. Fight that fight to your last breath. No mistake is the end of anyone's journey.

Self-indulgence is the biggest mistake. It is self-indulgent not to forgive yourself.

Stand back and counsel someone else. Hold their hand. Tell them there is always a future, a brighter future. If you do you will see your own solution.

It's called "getting on with getting on." Embrace the future.

You are forgiven.

Some One has died to make it so.

"Mortality"

Mortality kind of infers something permanent. It says we are mortal. What the heck does that mean? Whatever…

People die. Sure, what's the big deal? I am young enough and really busy Mister… go away. Obituary??? Who reads that? It's the last part of some stupid section in the paper. Everyone's pictures are just old people who died. Everybody dies. Go away… I am texting my friends.

Mortality means little unless you are old or you have seen someone die firsthand… You see its unfairness and you grasp its inevitability. If you do, your own life can gain focus and things (everything) become important. Being close to death makes life's meaning resplendent. Beauty is seen as not before. Beauty in the breath of a puppy or in the tears of a veteran or in the blush of the lover…

Mortality gives life meaning. Life you can resonate with if you look beyond the mirror. Young people are by nature dismissive and immature. It's ok, they have all the time in the world on their hands. Unless… they don't…

"Death is not fair."

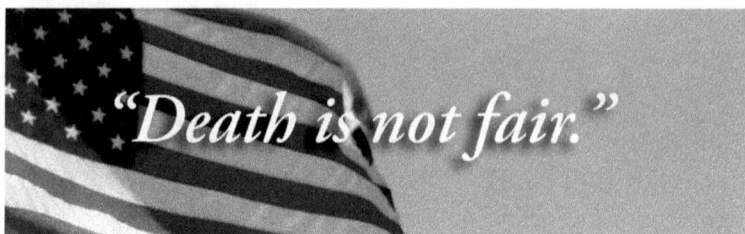

Death is not fair. Well, not fair when it is unexpected… but fair in that no one escapes it… Unless…??? Later…

I find it curious that the word morality is one letter short of mortality. I like to say that this letter "T" stands for Truth.

Truth is what morality is all about. Living in moral truth. Where do you find Truth? That is for you to explore and not quit until you have found it. The journey can take a lifetime. No one can do it for you.

Mortality takes on a new meaning in the shadow of morality. Mortality becomes a benign eventuality that beckons one to the next life. If you become truly and finally moral, death will not be feared. Death can be accepted and embraced.

Find out what Truth really is. You will be in awe of its simplicity. You will become at one with its humbling power.

Criticize and shun me all you want. The only thing that hurts is your pain.

Let me die for you.

"Opposition"

For every force there is an equal and opposite force. Newton says it is intrinsic to gravity and nature.

Is he saying that opposition is everywhere? There sure is opposition in politics. There sure is opposition in marriage. There sure is opposition even in church.

There are laws that we oppose. There are behaviors that we oppose. Who cannot be opposed to the abuse of child and woman?

As we start to move from childhood, to teens to 20's we find so may constrictions on our behavior. We don't like it and we react in opposition to anyone who will listen. Pity the poor parent. The problem with opposition is that it has become weak.

To the young "No" no longer means "No". It has become qualified with "maybe" and "if you are good." We have become experts at playing the "No" game and we are winning, though really losing...

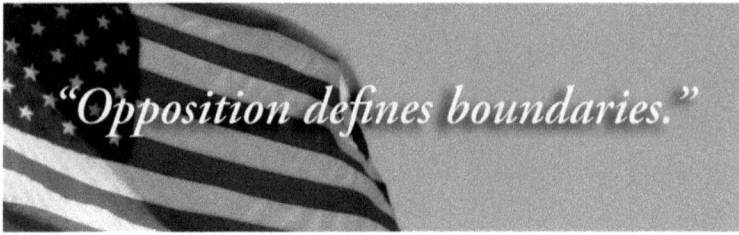

"Opposition defines boundaries."

Opposition defines boundaries. Life has real boundaries even though we think they don't exist or are not intended for us. Until… it is too late.

The opposition will wipe us out if our alcohol level is past code. Why do men come out of the military changed? Because they have met the invincibility of No, gimme 50's, or seen death. Opposition has reworked their manhood.

Today we are so sensitive about the sensitivities of others that we take their opposition as if it were the truth. We therefore enable them to believe that they are more right than we are. Today we are yielding to opposition. Our young hide behind their tweets and texts for self-affirmation. They avoid the "No's" of reality. Opposition is labeled as evil by the spineless.

Tear gas is fired into the crowds. Tears from tear gas hide the tears of vision and hope.

Opposition is painful but it teaches. It forces contemplation… then action when called for. It is the real "you" deep inside that must determine what you are in opposition of.

If you are opposed to nothing, then you are nobody.

Oppose evil. Oppose abuse. Oppose injustice. Oppose with your heart first… before your body.

Oppose with love and wisdom.

Hope you win this Super Bowl.

"The Arrogance of Me"

ME-Centric.

I could stop right now and leave it at that. That which defines the uniqueness (or malfunction?) of man... Or just the way that it is.

We all know that we are born and grow and see and feel and think with our own self. It is a miraculous journey. Maybe the greatest form of art there is. Girls morph into beauty and boys change into strength. Their uniqueness is forged in pain and softened by tears. Emotions are rampant during the formation process. This molding of uniqueness does not come without cost.

But uniqueness is the astounding miracle of life. How in the world are we all so different? Amazing. You don't even have to look into the heavens and the far galaxies to be overwhelmed with awe.

We all work hard at protecting the self. Our self. We pass through decades of insecurities and un-assuredness.

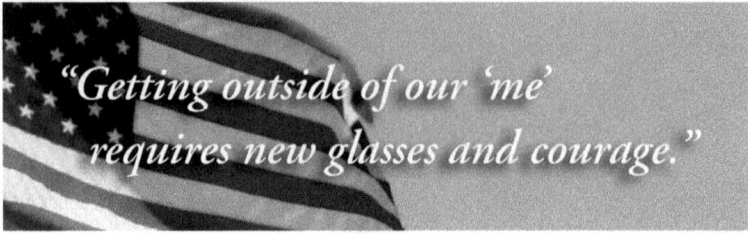

The focus goes inward. The protection of self requires defenses and walls. We become me-centric. Me first. It is subtle, but it drives action and words to be on the alert for intrusion and opposition. We become primarily defensive creatures. With this defensiveness comes sensitivity. We rail at criticism. Even comment becomes a possible threat. Withdrawal into sensitivity becomes our face and armor. They mirror our metaphorical kingdom. How do I look? How do I come across? Do they like me??

If this continues, then happiness becomes elusive and false substitutes are found… and addictions spawned.

There is one solution and it ain't "me." Getting outside of our "me" requires new glasses and courage. If it ain't "me" then it has to be "thee." Helping others is the only injection that will stop the spread of the "me" virus. The arrogance of me is deadly. It prevents humility. It prevents significance to society.

We have a hard time seeing that our pain or our mistakes are the key to helping others. Our uniqueness is formed in adversity and that adversity qualifies us to see the need in others and to help them. The sense of affirmation that comes from helping someone else is elemental to fulfillment and joy... and pride... and humility. This is the greatest porridge of life. Giving of self to others is the only menu worth serving. For many it takes a long time to realize this Truth. It is the purest form of Love. Not carnal but ethereal.

Go find someone in need, in pain and say, "Can I help you?" and then do it anyway.

Just do it.

You won't look back.

"What Next"

Why did I do that? Why do they do that? Nothing was accomplished! Or wasn't that great? I wish it could be that way all the time. Why is she so upset? Why is he so stupid? Why can't they just say nice things? Why does abuse exist? What is all this nonsense in the Middle East?

Aren't these some of the questions that ebb and flow in and out of our days? We could have so much fun continuing the list of them. And… sadly… it would be infinite. It is as if life is just a series of questions. The answers are in the past, but we have an aversion to looking over our shoulders… of using the past as a meaningful reference library for decision making. It requires work. We'd rather just go on hunches and feelings… down the old "I know what is best" path. History is for History class in school. Today it is biased to the politics of the teacher and writer. Truly, can we really trust even our sacrosanct Google for history? Through the eyes of whom?

"Light has to shine out of darkness."

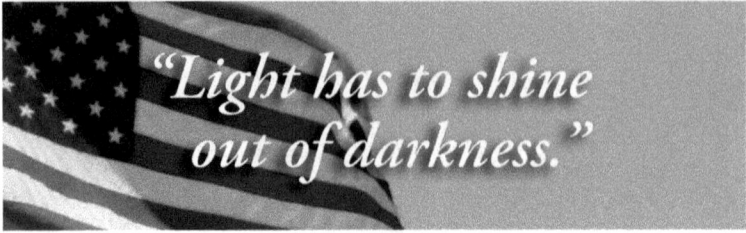

What next? How do we answer that question? How do we plan for the worst or the best? What next?

In Washington meetings are held by every agency to try to plan "what next". Every political party wants to know "what next". We talk about every possible scenario using our brains and those who can force any relevancy from the past to the decision at hand. Emotion and tension abound in the "what next" meetings.

Sadly, the arrogance of our intellect too often drives decisions which are not the best.

Our founding fathers had "what next" principles in mind when they carved out our Constitution's Bill of Rights. They were driven by realities from the past. They saw that freedom only came from morality and truth. Wow! Huuuhh? How could they be so smart?

Since then we have taken their "what next" and edited the morality part as it became more and more politically incorrect. We all know that we have to be so sensitive to the sensitivities of others that we are a jumble of indecision.

"What next?" is an even more frightening question if one is coming off injury, pain, abuse, or unfortunate circumstance. Everything is not for the good. Some stuff is just bad, sorry. But we can learn... Many of our greatest came from bad places.

We can learn only if we use the concept of "what next" as a tool to do only good, to seek out the Truth. Light has to shine out of darkness. If we feel abandoned then we must say we are NOT. We must believe in more than the pain or discomfort. To believe, you have to have Faith in something or faith in nothing. We have to make a choice. We can choose to live or we can choose to die. "What next" can be joyous if we just accept the past... discern the right and wrong... and charge forward with a positive and Faith-filled optimism. Surrounding ourselves with like-minded people who believe that values are important; who believe that serving others trumps serving self.

I challenge you not to give up on Faith. I did not say Church, I said Faith and... start looking up.

If you don't want to believe in Heaven it is your choice, but get out of my way. I am taking as many as I can on that boat... The Snow Goose.

What next, Paul? What next?

"The Grave"

Why does it happen? Why?

When we are young and vibrant our bodies do anything we ask of them. You can even become a SEAL. It seems like life is pain and pleasure, never to end. Love is sought and consumed. Truth is elusive and found often too late.

I just learned my golden retriever is dying five minutes ago. That is why I am writing this. His face and eyes are so vibrant as they penetrate your soul with trust and joy. He is old. He was our first dog in Maine... Well... he came in a crate from the Midwest on a truck. Certainly symbolic of humble beginnings. He lucked out as he got a great life with some other great dogs and a few great people. Unconditional love... where in the hell can you find it??? In his eyes for sure.

I was thinking that Heaven might allow us to rejoin with the spiritual essence of our pets and past. Would be nice... I am not talking about mom and dad or grandparents... just my dogs.

Gets you in your gut every time anything dies that is loved or appreciated…

Here I am thinking about existence… being defined by the grave.

If we all respected death maybe we could better respect life. Today there is little respect for anything. That is why I like the military as it teaches you respect, as do good parents, as do people who have the courage to say NO.

The grave can teach you everything you want to know, because at that time the eulogy is read and details how much the person accomplished, acquired, and enjoyed. Most eulogies are superficial as they talk about the material, not the spiritual essence of the individual.

Details that are important are not checks written, but time given to those who were hurting, to those in need. Were you a person who served the humblest or the mighty?

At the gravesite, where tears water the new sod, is the truth. Read the words reflected in the tears and you may find out who you were.

Goodbye my dear friend. Goodbye Kenne.

May He soon pat you on the head...

"Fine Gold"

14 kt.

Just the sound of that rings true. That has universal value. I mean universal. It also looks fantastic. There is nothing like gold jewelry. Celebrities and the wealthy flaunt it whenever they can. Designers put their twist on it and charge even more. You have 14kt and you are a member of the club. No need to worry about self-image. 14 kt is fine gold and it makes you fine.

Now that we have finally agreed on what is truly important we can take a deep breath and relax.

Why is this funny looking shiny gold metal worth so much to us? In time of trouble or uncertainty we flock toward it making it even more valuable. It is hidden and hoarded as the ultimate protection short of a gun. It makes us feel safe.

We put our eggs in this basket.

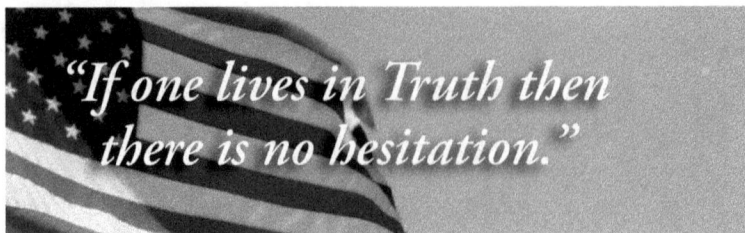

But, there is something even more valuable than gold. It is called the Truth. We don't play games with gold but we do with the Truth. We are the hypocrites. We are experts at shading the Truth. The white lie is on the throne.

I have finally learned that the Truth, and telling it to others, makes life rich and joyous. If one lives in Truth then there is no hesitation, facts are once again facts, and bureaucracies diminish in size by 50%. Wow… This is amazing. Of course, some of the negative fallout is a reduction of crime, theft, abuse and dishonesty. All the fine gold in the world can't do that.

But, we idiots continue to disrespect Truth. We put our own slants on it. We are critics of others who have the courage to speak the Truth. Truth is black and white. It is universal. Truth begets compassion. 14 kt doesn't. We are sick because we have turned our backs on truth and devalued it.

Why do kids like adults who tell the Truth?

Because they know what we no longer know.

"The Victim"

The Victim.

This is the role most people choose. We are born of good parents or complicated parental circumstances. We are raised with love and discipline or chaos. Good things happen to some, bad things happen to others. If you are born in the USA you may be luckier... but you can also live the pain of the Third World in our own economic third world.

Then you can find a stimulating job, no job, or a bureaucratic CYA job. You can be murdered by political correctness or diminished by your own attitudes. You can feel entitled or opportunistic.

Then you age and look back on what you could have done or marvel at what you have.

Most like the "glass is half full" philosophy. Most want to hide behind the skirt of the "victim." When you are the victim it is easy to criticize and blame others. The problem

is that it gets you nowhere, absolutely nowhere... Blame is a cancer... though you feel in control.

Everyone is a hypocrite but you. Except that the opposite is the truth.

Enjoy your Victim Complex. It is a sinking ship.

Now, for the sake of humor, let's consider the Victor Complex. Both are VC's... nice, eh? Hard to tell them apart. See... the stupid person who chooses to be a victor never gives up, never blames, never compromises. This person has core values. This person is never politically correct. This person is never unhappy unless someone is hurt by untruth and unfairness. But then this is seized as an opportunity to attack the injustice... With no fear of self-consequences.

Who is this person?

This is the person who is less concerned with self than the well-being of others. That is all that matters. It can be lonely and painful as few will understand. But too bad. This is the road of the Victor.

In my "hide" I await with patience the reveal of selfishness and quietly squeeze the truth trigger.

Who do you want to be? The Victim or the Victor?

Your choice. Think about it. A lot…

"The Last Chapter"

What do we want our last chapter to be? What do I want this last chapter to be? I have no clue right now... as I did most of my life. Life is so intense and exciting and painful and absorbing that who has the time to think or care about their last chapter? We all think we are books with no last page. I won't ever be on oxygen or on life support... Not me. Too much going on right now. Excited about cooking steaks tonight...

The last chapter has to be good... you need to finish reading it with a sigh and a whew... "That was really something"... others need to reflect on your life the same way... I sure hope they aren't saying "What a jerk!" under their breaths. You mean I can't take all my stuff and money with me? To the majority of the world it was an exhausting, painful, and lonely journey... The last chapter being welcomed as a relief. Third World injustice and poverty abroad and also right here... Abuse endured by children, family, and by women. Inexplicable. Damned inexplicable.

> *"Self-centrism is the accepted and promoted solution to unhappiness."*

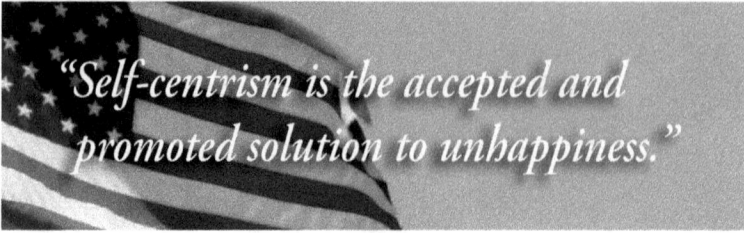

The last chapter is when you look back on your life with the wisdom of time and experience. Most will say it makes no sense. But then if nothing makes sense... then values become irrelevant. Good, evil... just words. Money... the only solution and source of happiness. Everything is defined by it or lack thereof. A philosophy of money. It is the religion of the enlightened. I choose to say "nonsense"... And "too bad"... your choice and your insignificance confirmed.

Last chapters should be true celebrations of the good that has been fought for and achieved... good that is cradled in humility and selflessness. There should be lines of people you have helped applauding... and hopefully some you have hurt maybe forgiving...

Maybe 50% of what you leave should be given to family and 50% to the poor. Maybe the government should stay out of it.

There once was a man named Paul several thousand years ago. He was a real jerk. He hurt and killed a lot of people. His last chapter should have been hell. But he met Someone who inspired him. Who shamed him by His innocence and Truth. The Embodiment of Good. Once filled with His Spirit he could now only go down one path. His past was shameful, to say the least. But he knew he was forgiven if he chose to do only good. Doing good and talking about it back then was very dangerous. One would be scorned and mocked… as good was politically incorrect. Evil and self were co-mingled and lives lost.

Sound familiar? Self-centrism is the accepted and promoted solution to unhappiness. This is really hard to fight as media and politics have usurped individual mandate. Government regulations obscure fairness and the self-correcting potential of society. Even race has become a political football, a game played by activists and Washington. Christian ethos has been denigrated. Labels are used to diminish the courageous who say values should rule. Schools cannot teach values. Sensitivity to sensitivity is the new indulgent cancer... Our Constitution is labeled as being outdated. The Bill of Rights is being expanded to mean everything has rights, even evil. God is being deleted from our past. God is being accused of being bad. God is being taken off buildings. Prayer is labeled as divisive unless you are facing East.

My Last Chapter is titled "God Bless You" and "Hurry Back Jesus". We need the drug of your Holy Spirit now.

I have been blessed with a journey that has not seen the real poverty or felt the real pain of the majority. Please don't judge me by the immaterial, much less the material. I was born in Bronxville, NY in 1940. Grew up in Louisville and St Louis. Graduated from Yale and went into the Navy. I had the great honor of fulfilling my dream to become a Frogman. I graduated from BUDS Class 31E, Basic Underwater Demolition/Seal School. I was an officer in Underwater Demolition Team 21 which became Seal Team 4 in 1984. I had the honor of recovering several spacecraft, including Gemini 6/7 & AS-201, the very first Apollo Spacecraft to go into space. Wow, did I luck out. Then I spent 40 years in women's retail, in various department stores. Even a year at the World Wrestling Federation... go figure?

I have two great daughters and two grandchildren who have just discovered the water and facemasks. My wife has created probably the #1 women's accessory store in the country as evidenced by how much she is copied. Therein I work and report to her... No comment. LOL.

As you can tell by reading between the lines there is a spiritual side to my journey. Kind of covert as I just want to make a difference unseen.

God Bless You All… Happy Trails.

ACKNOWLEDGEMENTS

Families matter more than ever.

They are being torn apart by politics.

Our grandchildren and great-great grandchildren are looking to us to show them the path to Truth....

Please read every chapter privately, please....

My short list of contributors:

My daughters, Candice and Courtney, who have much more to learn about their dad. There is my brilliant wife Christina who continued to inadvertently mold me. And there are my friends from the past whose life journeys I do not fully know, and who do not know me now. For in life we are who we become, not who we were.

Then there are the men of my "No Walls" Bible Studies, and Max Lucado who freed us to think with assurance and humility, leading me to new friendships of the highest quality. Durrenberger, Lord, Wood among many others.

There are the veterans I served with and those I didn't: Ames, Riojas, Stevens, Cleary, Cofield, Diviney, Bisset,

Shapira, Fry, Ross, Hawes, Hawkins, Heaphy, Hernandez, Bruton, Olson, Vecchione, Phillips, Waddel, Blais, Sutherland, and my brothers in UDT/R BUD/S 31E and countless others…. Where bonding and trust was defined.

Lastly, there is Sandra Simmons-Dawson, President of Customer Finder Marketing, who helped edit and format the books, website, and marketing.

Chris Bent

Naples
September 2013
www.chrisbent.com

IN THE WORDS OF OTHERS

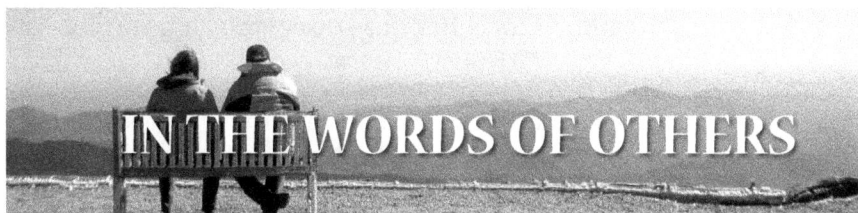

"This is a book by a man of many directions and passions. Straightforward yet thought provoking. Loyal to his convictions and country. And brave. Sharing. Warrior. Humanitarian."

Jeff Lytle, Editorial Page Editor, Naples Daily News

"As a friend, Chris has helped me understand the inherent conflicts embedded in the language of 'political correctness' and how it attempts, and frequently succeeds, in disguising and defeating the 'truth.' Chris is engaged in a rhetorical battle — we need his insight."

William Lord, a 32-year-veteran Executive Producer
and Vice-President of ABC News, and
Professor of Journalism at Boston University

"Chris writes like he lives. As a man of distinction, he is a voice for the poor, a champion of the truth and a friend of strong character and conviction. His word and his service are a blessing to all who encounter him."

Vann R. Ellison, President/CEO, St. Matthew's House, Inc.

"My nickname for Chris is "Dream-Catcher"- because that's who he is to me. He is my mentor in how to give on His behalf. Freely and generously, Chris offers both words, "God bless you!", and gifts. And all the while he is making a compelling and powerful statement. Chris Bent has discovered a beautiful way to live!"

Rev. Dr. Ruth Merriam, The Church on the Cape (U.M.C.), Cape Porpoise, Maine — Chris's 'other' pastor!

"Chris Bent is a very unusual person – Navy SEAL, Yale graduate, successful business owner, and radical Christian who is comfortable talking with anyone at any level in society. He doesn't just talk about faith or caring about the poor, Chris actually lives his faith and he works with the poor. His smile is genuine and reflects his deep joy in life, America, hard work, people and (most definitely) God. I have enjoyed reading his writings; they are different, often hard hitting and sometimes maybe even a little wild. Each one gives a fresh perspective on contemporary lives, reflecting Chris' intelligence and faith. Chris enjoys moving mountains."

Rev. Dr. Ted Sauter, Senior Pastor, North Naples United Methodist Church

www.ingramcontent.com/pod-product-compliance
Lightning Source LLC
Chambersburg PA
CBHW050112280326
41933CB00010B/1070